Praise for *Inside the Miracle*

"In *Inside the Miracle,* Mark Nepo gathers almost thirty years of writing, teaching, and thinking about suffering, healing, and wholeness, drawing on his own transformative experience with illness. With everyday lessons and hard-earned wisdom, he has given us a beautiful testament to the resilience of the human heart, and a guide to facing life's challenges with strength, grace, and gratitude."
ARIANNA HUFFINGTON
author of *Thrive*

"*Inside the Miracle* is simply the best book I have read in years. Mark Nepo invites us to live a human life—fully, joyously, and without reservation, using all our experiences and vulnerabilities as a precious opportunity to encounter and serve the Mystery. He has blessed us all."
RACHEL NAOMI REMEN, MD
author of *Kitchen Table Wisdom* and *My Grandfather's Blessings*

"*Inside the Miracle* will be a miracle for those who read it, especially those going through a difficult time, a big change, a loss, a confusion, a trial by fire. That means everyone born human. Our trials may differ in heat and length, but at the core, we are the same. We need each other, we need insight, and we need help. This book is help. It helps me every time I pick it up and read a poem or a teaching or the brave story of Mark Nepo's descent and rebirth."
ELIZABETH LESSER
cofounder of Omega Institute and author of
Broken Open: How Difficult Times Can Help Us Grow

"A sensitive sharing of the truth. I recommend it highly."
BERNIE SIEGEL, MD
author of *Love, Medicine & Miracles*

"In the canyon of his soul, scoured into truth by pain and uncertainty, joy and Mystery, Nepo navigates the deeper currents with prose and poetry that masterfully invites us into those places where only rarely language can reach. Relentlessly refusing to resolve paradox into mere piety, this book is a rare soul-confirming and soul-stretching gift."

SHARON DALOZ PARKS
author of *Big Questions, Worthy Dreams*

"With a hard-won heart, Mark Nepo takes us inside the miracle of our radiant and fragile human life. In every page, Mark reveals the universal in the personal, intimating the wholeness that is best expressed in paradox. This book is raw and painful and indestructibly hopeful. It tells us what we already know in fresh and surprising moments of recognition. This is a gift which we can open endlessly."

BRUCE TIFT
author of *Already Free*

"A moving testament to the human spirit."

JON KABAT-ZINN
author of *Wherever You Go, There You Are*

"Amazingly honest and inspiring for those confronting serious illness or dramatic transitions . . . Nepo's message is for everyone."

LIBRARY JOURNAL STARRED REVIEW

"'God, Self and Medicine' and 'Troubled Waters' are ground-breaking, compassionate essays that achieve an epic majesty."

HERBERT MASON
professor emeritus of history and religious thought
at Boston University and translator of *Gilgamesh*

"Deep optimism is when you can still see—through the darkness of illness, despair, death, and injustice—the single light that illuminates the world. Mark never loses touch with that source. That is his gift. These essays, a collection of jewels, are his gifts to the rest of us . . . Mark Nepo is a rare being, a poet who does not overuse language, a wise man without arrogance, a teacher who always speaks with compassion, and an easygoing love-to-listen-to-him storyteller . . ."

JAMES FADIMAN, PHD
author of *The Other Side of Haight*
and coauthor of *Essential Sufism*

PRAISE FOR MARK NEPO

"Mark Nepo is one of the finest spiritual guides of our time."

PARKER J. PALMER
author of *A Hidden Wholeness* and *The Courage to Teach*

"Mark Nepo is a Great Soul. His resonant heart—and his frank and astonishing voice—befriend us mightily on this mysterious trail."

NAOMI SHIHAB NYE
author of *You and Yours, 19 Varieties of Gazelle:
Poems of the Middle East,* and *Red Suitcase*

"Mark Nepo is an eloquent spiritual teacher."

HERBERT MASON
professor emeritus of history and religious thought
at Boston University and translator of *Gilgamesh*

"Mark Nepo joins a long tradition of truth-seeking, wild-hearted poets—Rumi, Walt Whitman, Emily Dickinson, Mary Oliver— and deserves a place in the center of the circle with them."

ELIZABETH LESSER
cofounder of Omega Institute and author of
Broken Open: How Difficult Times Can Help Us Grow

"Mark Nepo's work is as gentle and reliable as the tides, and as courageous as anyone I've known in looking deeply into the mysteries of the self."

MICHAEL J. MAHONEY
author of *Human Change Processes*

"Nepo is a consummate storyteller with a rare gift for making the invisible visible."

PUBLISHERS WEEKLY

INSIDE THE
MIRACLE

ALSO BY MARK NEPO

NONFICTION
The Endless Practice
Seven Thousand Ways to Listen
Finding Inner Courage
Unlearning Back to God
The Exquisite Risk
The Book of Awakening

FICTION
As Far As the Heart Can See

POETRY
Reduced to Joy
Surviving Has Made Me Crazy
Suite for the Living
Inhabiting Wonder
Acre of Light
Fire Without Witness
God, the Maker of the Bed, and the Painter

EDITOR
Deepening the American Dream

RECORDINGS
Inside the Miracle (expanded edition, 2015)
Reduced to Joy
The Endless Practice
Seven Thousand Ways to Listen
Staying Awake
Holding Nothing Back
As Far As the Heart Can See
The Book of Awakening
Finding Inner Courage
Finding Our Way in the World
Inside the Miracle (1996)

INSIDE THE MIRACLE

MIRACLE

ENDURING SUFFERING,
APPROACHING WHOLENESS

Mark Nepo

sounds true
BOULDER, COLORADO

Sounds True
Boulder, CO 80306

Sounds True is a trademark of Sounds True, Inc.

Published 2015

Cover design by Jennifer Miles
Book design by Beth Skelley

Printed in the United States of America

Library of Congress Cataloging-in-Publication Data
Nepo, Mark.
  Inside the miracle : enduring suffering approaching wholeness / Mark Nepo.
    pages cm
  ISBN 978-1-62203-491-8—ISBN 978-1-62203-554-0 (Ebook)
  1. Cancer—Patients—Religious life. 2. Suffering—Religious aspects. 3. Nepo, Mark.
  4. Miracles. 5. Healing—Religious aspects. I. Title.
  BL625.9.S53N47 2015
  204›.42—dc23
                              2015013399

Ebook ISBN 978-1-62203-554-0

10 9 8 7 6 5 4 3 2 1

for any spirit
suddenly awakened
to how deep its life
how short its stay

CONTENTS

APPROACHING WHOLENESS

STILL HERE, STILL WONDERING

Upon Seeking Tu Fu as a Guide

And so I asked him, how is it God is everywhere and nowhere? He circled me like a self I couldn't reach, "Because humans refuse to live their lives." I was confused. He continued, "You hover rather than enter." I was still confused. He spoke in my ear, "God is only visible within your moment entered like a burning lake." I grew frightened. He laughed, "Even now, you peer at me as if what you see and hear are not a part of you." I grew angry. He ignored me, "You peer at the edge of your life, so frantic to know, so unwilling to believe." Indeed, I was frantic. He was in my face, "And now that you have cancer, you ask to be spared." I grew depressed. He took my shoulders, "For God's sake! Enter your own life! Enter!"

TO MY READER

One of the great transforming passages in my life was having cancer in my mid-thirties. This experience unraveled the way I see the world. It scoured my lens of perception, landing me in a deeper sense of living. There are certain experiences that reform us, as if God's a tireless blacksmith who, against our pleading, forges the metal in us, though it takes years for our heart and mind to cool from the pounding. My journey with cancer was how I was forged.

One of the mysteries of being human is that healing is a process that never ends. Transformation, even from a single event, can continue for Eternity. And so, I continue to be transformed by my journey with cancer, which began with my struggle through three years of illness and alarm from 1987 to 1990. All those years ago, that struggle brought me close to death. Today, I remain committed to surfacing the lessons of transformation as they continue to shape the lens that life has given me. The transformative events may differ for each of us, but every soul will face a life-changing threshold that will keep shaping who we are for the rest of our life.

I felt compelled to expand this book because almost dying and having cancer cracked my life open and continues to deepen who I am. I felt compelled to rework and further unfold these life lessons as my understanding keeps evolving. I felt uplifted to add new lessons from the growing perspective of decades. And so, this book gathers twenty-eight years of my writing and teaching about suffering, healing, and wholeness.

It's important to admit that I'm not the same person at sixty-four as when first diagnosed at thirty-six. In my thirties, I was a driven artist, obedient to a relentless muse, while addicted to working in the world for approval. I was a dedicated and loyal friend but mostly inflamed with a vision I couldn't quite articulate. My understanding of life was way ahead of my ability to live life. So cancer stopped me, humbled me, frightened me, threw me off course, turned me upside down and inside out. I was suddenly on God's anvil, being hammered and reshaped. And everything that had worked to that point—my dedication, my attention to detail, my perseverance, my certainty in my muse—all of that was shattered and of no use. I was terrified and lost.

During that time, I endured a horribly botched first chemo treatment in New York City that left me squatting on the floor of a Holiday Inn with my former wife Ann and my dear old friend Paul. It was three weeks after having a rib removed from my back, and I was throwing up every twenty minutes till I began to cough up blood. It was at that moment in the weak grey before dawn that Ann, in her fear and pain, cried out, "Where is God?" Slouched in a corner, I somehow whispered, "Here, right here." I don't know where such an understanding came from. In truth, all the books I've written over the years and all the teaching circles I've convened have been an endless attempt to understand what came to me in that moment. This book tries to gather some of what I've learned along the way.

As coal is pressed into a diamond, experience presses us into the clear jewel that we are. Difficult as this is, this is the hard-earned way that wisdom appears in the world. And though what's unearthed here comes from the heat of my journey, the lessons are for everyday living. It's a law of spiritual nature: that the press of crisis, illness, heartbreak, and grief make visible what's essential to live. Somehow, our life-giving lessons are more easily seen through the press of difficulty. So much of what we learn and pass on is the residue of more heated times. This is how we preserve what matters. This is how we create medicine out of our suffering.

THE JOURNEY

When my former wife and I were both stricken with cancer, the months became a labyrinth. In May of '87, Ann was diagnosed as having cervical cancer in situ. This led to her having a conization in June and a hysterectomy that August. While she was healing, I had a mysterious lump forming on my head, which turned out to be growing underneath the skull as well. It grew to the size of half a grapefruit. And so, mere days after her surgery, I entered the hospital, moving through a gauntlet of tests, including an open biopsy, which diagnosed this strange lesion as a lymphoma lodged between my brain and skull. It was eating through the bone.

During this time, I was unable to find my bearings, had no sense of center, and was unsure about everything. But in the center of my terror, there was a small voice stirring, emanating, and building from under all my trouble. It didn't speak in words, and I was unaccustomed to listening for it or to it. I know now it came from the core of all life and all time and began to assert itself through the bottom of my personality, the way sunlight passes through a crack in a barn. This was my first feeling of the touchstone of grace that would grow and lessen my terror over time.

As I struggled between my fear of procedures and surgeries and my attempts to listen for that touchstone of grace growing inside me, I began to be visited in dream by the great Chinese poet Tu Fu, a loving, authentic spirit from the Tang Dynasty who spoke plainly about the pains and wonders of living. This was my first experience of forces we could call guides. No one can prove their existence. But as fish can feel the current move them along, we can feel the current of life move us along. During times of suffering, we're invited to listen more deeply for the current of life, no matter how it appears. It may come as a memory of your beloved grandmother long gone or in the voice of a Chinese poet from the 700s. When suffering, we're challenged to accept help however it appears.

By October, after months of desperation, and prayer, and visualization, and the appearance of guides, and fighting with and against doctors, the tumor—both below the skull and above—vanished, avoiding major brain surgery, whole-head radiation, and spinal chemotherapy.

The doctors could not explain it, and our friends and family helped us limp back to life, a struggle in itself, which we were shaping strongly until a year later, in November of '88, a spot on my eighth rib began to grow. We were crushed.

By the following January, a lump protruded on my back. In February of '89, I underwent thoracic surgery to remove that rib and its adjacent muscles. The cells in that rib were clearly malignant, and so, barely repaired, I embarked on four months of chemotherapy. Today, as of my last checkup, I am well and forever changed.

I had, quite frankly, found death at my shoulder earlier than most. Yet I had also been touched by a relentless, mysterious grace, which surfaced briefly to restore me. Now, I find myself tied to a fathomless place where I had not dared to voyage. I call that reservoir God, though you may call it something else.

Though my story is framed around a particular crisis, I believe that all forms of crisis somehow raise a common instinct to survive, and with that a common set of tools—such as risk, trust, compassion, and surrender—becomes available to all. And coming this far, it seems clear that being a survivor is embracing the will to live, and whether that embrace lasts for years or months or days or even hours, whoever embraces life *is* a survivor.

Sooner or later, we're asked to be honest with our fears and hopes, to render, through our experience, the irreducible mystery of life in which we all swim. After all this way, I know that I am weak and strong, stubborn and determined, afraid and brave, giving and demanding, resilient and stalled, confused and clear—sometimes all at once. I know now that going on without denying any aspect of the human drama is what strength is all about.

We'd been on fire and almost burned to death, only to be tossed more deeply into the ocean of life, where we almost drowned. Now, we were cast ashore, to start over and find our way, which was a difficult blessing all by itself, one we ultimately couldn't do together.

It was four years later that Ann and I divorced. It was no one's fault. When a large stone falls into a lake, the water around it is sent in all directions away from the point of impact. Events like cancer are such large stones crashing from nowhere into the water of our lives. If you happen to be on the same side of the point of impact, you might be propelled in a similar direction. But sometimes, as with Ann and I, the cancer landed right between us and we were propelled in opposite directions into the rest of our lives. From all these years later, it's humbling to realize the power and aftershock of cancer or any life-changing experience. While no longer in close contact, we helped save each other's lives. And so, all there is to say is thank you, even to the unspeakable thing that crashed into our lives.

A Story That Continues to Be Written

During the heat and fire of this journey, I wrote in a journal. I wasn't trying to create art or craft anything. I was reduced to a life of expression that was helping me to live. While struggling to be here, I never thought of putting any of this into a book. It was a few years later, while drifting back into the stream of life, that I felt a need to bear witness to the journey I'd been through and to give voice to the common experience I'd been exposed to. What I'd endured was the journey that everyone endures, in different circumstances and with different names.

In 1994, I self-published a small fifty-seven-page edition of this book under the title *Acre of Light: Living with Cancer.* That early edition quickly sold out. Two years later, Ithaca House Books, a small press in upstate New York, offered to publish a second edition. Later that same year, Parabola published the first audio version of the book, under the title *Inside the Miracle: Enduring Illness, Approaching Wholeness.* The master tape took a week to record on reel-to-reel in a studio near Lincoln Center in New York City. It resulted in two intimate audiocassettes, which *Publishers Weekly* named as one of the best audiotapes of the year.

We originally recorded the Parabola edition to make it available to those who could no longer read in the roughness of their journey. We were humbled to learn that the book and the audio program had a far greater reach. The lessons surfaced by the acuteness of being ill proved useful to everyone in the bump and flare of their ordinary days. This is why I've changed the subtitle in this edition from *Enduring Illness* to *Enduring Suffering.* Because, ill or not, everyone experiences suffering of some kind that we each have to endure. The stories and lessons here are for everyone.

Those original editions, published twenty-one years ago, have long since gone out of print. And I'm deeply glad that this work is available again in this expanded form. So what you have in your hands is a thematically integrated work that draws from three sources that span almost three decades of writing: the original poems and prose from *Inside the Miracle* (1994, 1996, now out of print); ten relevant essays from my collected personal essays, *Unlearning Back to God* (2006, now out of print); and thirty-nine new poems and prose pieces not yet published. While I've put all this together in the arc of a life's journey, the book is not chronological, but follows an inward evolution. I've also let each piece remain in the present tense and mood of when I wrote it, to preserve the immediacy of the experience.

A Story That Continues to Be Lived

We are each in a lifetime conversation with suffering and care that, in time, will open us to our strengths and gifts. We are meant, it seems, to come apart and come together, so we can discover who we are at the core. We are meant, it seems, to be rearranged by what we go through and held up to that process by those who care. We are meant to accept suffering and care as our teachers, our mentors, as the tools used by time to shape us into what matters.

And while we each want a map for how to live our lives, your map won't help me and my map won't guide you. Only inhabiting our personhood can reveal our map to us. All we can do is encourage each other to enliven our personal authenticity, which will lead us to discover and decipher our own way. So sharing the raw truth of my journey is only meant as an encouragement, not as a guide. Ultimately, we each are meant to gather meaning through relationship: with ourselves, each other, and with suffering and care.

Through the years, we are ever changed and changing. Even as I write this, the teachers of suffering and care are shaping me further. During the last year, I lost my father at ninety-three, a man I loved who I was estranged from along the way and close to at the end. And after thirteen years, my wife Susan and I lost our beloved dog-child Mira, a yellow lab whose immediate and unfaltering love taught us much. These deep losses have thrown me into my latest conversation with suffering and care, through which I continue to grow more salient and tender. So, even though I thought this book was done, I felt compelled to include lessons from these losses. If any of these stories touch your story, it's because the particular sufferings and care we each encounter place us in the story of all suffering and care. And in that sea lives our resilience.

How to Use This Book

This book itself is a journey, not offered in a straight line but quite circuitous—because that is how life is. Though events happen sequentially through the years, their impact gathers and merges inwardly. This is the inner rhythm of healing that leads to wholeness. My healing journey keeps reverberating forward, backward, sideways, and back to the beginning, always different but at heart the same. The journey of this book tries to introduce you to this mysterious process.

So the book does not need to be read in order. You can feel free to move about the chapters and poems, to linger with what touches or challenges you, to stay in conversation with whatever lights your heart. I encourage you to clear a path to your own sense of meaning. Toward that end, I invite you to keep a journal. You may, when moved, find it helpful to take a break, go for a walk, to enter your journal, or discuss a story or feeling that has arisen with a friend.

Often, when speaking of the all-encompassing Mystery of the Universe and the Oneness of Things, I capitalize the largest energies of life that can only be pointed to. When I refer to the Whole of Life or the Spirit that informs our lives, I am honoring at once the ineffable forces that are particular for each of us and yet common to all of us.

This book is also a weaving of prose and poetry. So let me say a word about the nature of poetry. Poetry is the unexpected utterance of the soul. Such deep utterances are teachers that help us make the journey from our head to our heart. For me, the poems arrive with their wisdom. I retrieve them, more than create them, and they become my guides. What they have to say becomes my inner curriculum and, by staying in conversation with the poems, I learn and grow. Whether you write or not, this way of learning is available to us all, as we meet and learn from the moments of our lives. Whether familiar with poetry or not, I invite you to receive the poems as you would a friend who's eager to share intimately. Let the feeling reach you first. For the purpose of a poem is to awaken your own feeling.

Throughout the book, you will also encounter *Questions to Walk With.* These are journal questions, invitations to be in conversation with yourself, and table questions, invitations to be in conversation with a friend or loved one—each as a way to personalize the common passages in life, and to explore where the lessons and challenges live in you. Please, use and develop the questions you're drawn to; change them and share them as you're moved.

Let me also say a few words about journaling. In exploring these questions, try not to select what to write about. Instead, try to open your heart and mind, by meditating on the question in silence for a minute or two, and see what wants your heart's attention. Once writing, don't censor what arises. These expressions are for you. It's more important to be honest with yourself than to hold back because someone else might see what you write. Don't worry about being organized or making sense, or even if you write in full sentences. Let your heart and deeper mind be your guide. And please remember, these exercises are experiments in authenticity. There is no right or wrong way to do this, no normal amount of time each takes, and no one way to surface what you feel.

We're now at the threshold of the one journey we all share. As we enter, it's my hope that the trail of this lifetime conversation with suffering and care will open you to the fullness of your own humanity. With a steadfast belief in our aliveness, I hope what's here will help you meet the transformation that waits in however you're being forged.

Enduring Suffering

In life one plays the hand one is dealt to the best of one's ability. Those who insist on playing, not the hand they were given, but the one they insist they should have been dealt—these are life's failures. We are not asked if we will play. That is not an option. Play we must. The option is how.

ANTHONY DE MELLO

*I*t's snowing in March, and the large flakes are drifting every which way looking for a home, each as fragile as a life on Earth trying to find its place in the mysterious swirl and flow that has gone on forever. And to its surprise, each flake falling from the sky lands and merges with the Earth, becoming part of what's foundational. This too is our fate. We're tossed into life, headlong and heartlong, into swirls of fragility, which eventually merge us with all that's foundational. Of course, there's pain and fear and worry along the way, even times of despair when all we know seems so very close to being erased. But hard as it is, being erased is part of the incubation of all that's substantial. When erased of our assumptions and conclusions, we're returned to the innocence of childhood. This is how we begin again. I have found myself in all these phases, more than once: waking suddenly in mid-fall from the sky, feeling more fragile than I could bear, afraid my very self will be erased, only to land and merge with the thing that outlasts us all. Such moments of joining can stun us into a turn of resilience. No one can guide us through this process. We can only bear witness that it's possible, even probable.

The pieces in this section are personal accounts of this mysterious and arduous journey, in and out of being half-hearted and whole-hearted, in and out of feeling ill and feeling well, in and out of fearing death and welcoming rebirth. Most of these pieces were written in my thirties and early forties. The essays here unfold what I saw when closest to death. In "God, Self, and Medicine," I discovered how the part is always in relationship to the Whole, whether we acknowledge this kinship or not. In "A Terrible Knowledge," I discovered the paradox of suffering and the necessity of feeling in order to move through our suffering. And in "Dance of the Seed," I discovered the puncture of grief and the endless proliferation of life that reseeds itself once we, as its carrier, are gone. The poems in this section are raw accounts of my confusion of what to do with my will, where to place it, and when it made no difference. The poems explore the hard gift of waiting and letting go, and how my suffering forever opened me to the suffering of others.

All of these pieces offer a sense of what it means to endure, a sense of what's necessary in order to face, experience, and enliven the life we're given.

Each of us must enhance our inner skills if we're to live a full life: how to be whole-hearted, how to face death and welcome rebirth, how to stay in relationship to the Whole, how to inhabit the necessity of feeling in order to move through our suffering, how to withstand the puncture of grief until it reveals the proliferation of life, how to learn what to do with our will and when to surrender, and how to accept the hard gift of waiting and letting go. Our experience with these qualities forms our personal practice of enduring.

GOD, SELF, AND MEDICINE

S

ince long before the story of Job, human beings, the
most fragile and durable of all species, have had to deal
with the paradox of suffering. And in our pain we ache to know,
if there is a God, how can that eternal presence sanction pain
and breakage, and further, in the face of all this, how can such
an all-knowing force fuel us with the capacity and sensitivity to
suffer so acutely. From the young slave crushed by a stone headed
for the top of a pyramid to the senseless shooting of a clerk in
Detroit, those left to grieve have asked in Universal echo *why*, as
the rest of us stand in silent chorus voicing a bewildered hymn
that has lasted centuries.

It is no mistake that to suffer means *to feel keenly, to undergo
experience.* As we flex our knot of blood, which some call heart,
we're blessed and cursed to stumble through the searing moments
that both threaten and enrich our lives. For to feel keenly is the
only path to transformation and wholeness, if it doesn't kill us
first. Just like the stubborn rocks along the ocean, the pounding
of the deep, in time, will reveal an inner beauty otherwise
hidden, if we can endure the scouring. But we are not rocks. Our
acuteness of perception and inner sensation, our unprecedented
range of thought and mood, make us so vulnerable that we can
die and be reborn daily, an emotional form of Prometheus. So our
continual quest is to stay more renewed than devoured; our chief
task, to find a way to gain enough from what is revealed to survive
the pain of such opening.

That's the point of engaging our experience: to gain enough
from what we feel to survive the pain in feeling it, to live through
the thresholds that paradox offers, to live through the pain of
breaking to the other side, into the rearrangement of nothing

less than our very lives. In truth, we don't have to seek this sort of experience. We can't avoid it. We somehow have to find the courage to feel the days keenly.

My breaking has, indeed, led me into an expanding love of being that is clearly God. I have been broken by disease and know fully that there are moments endured from which our lives will never be the same, severe moments beyond which everything is changed. No one asks for these moments. They simply happen the way a merciless wind cracks a tree we never imagined would crack.

I know now, that being human, we are each the crucible, the ever-changing inlet through which the greater Whole in all its forms ebbs and flows. Indeed, every time the Universe, through Nature or God, flows through us, we are rinsed larger, cleansed and charged again. What is medicine, if not the laws of nature applied to cleanse the self? And what is God, if not the laws of Spirit applied to enlarge the self? It implies that to enlarge is cleansing; to grow, healing. In this way, to talk about the art of healing is to investigate the various ways, both natural and spiritual, that the Whole, if taken in, can preserve the part.

~ ~ ~

Until my cancer diagnosis, I'd never been ill. I was terrified, and nothing was helping me conquer the fear. Initially, I felt a traumatic paralysis, the fast breathing, huddled fear of a wounded animal lying still in the brush, expecting to be struck again. This is worse than outright pain, this is withdrawing from anything that can help. This is the power of fear—to make us recoil from anything larger. While in this state, nothing flows through, and therefore, nothing cleanses or enlarges. The center remains cut off when it needs to be renewed more than ever. My life has taught me that how we first stand after doubling over is crucial to whether we will heal at all.

In time, I was broken of my illusion that fear could be conquered. Instead, I began to watch the winter trees as they let the wind through, always through. Since then, I've learned that fear gets its power from not looking, that it's intensified by isolation, that it's always more strident when we are self-centered. Now, when I am full of fear, which can't be avoided, I try, though I don't always succeed, to break its stridency by breaking my egocentrism. I try to quiet its intensity by admitting my fear to loved ones, and I try to disempower its exaggeration by looking directly into exactly what I fear. I try to know that though I can be fearful, I am more than my fear.

But life under siege hides none of its difficulties. The endless decisions that must be made, each imperative and of great consequence, do not wait for us to manage our fear. Indeed, one is always *thrust* into the world of cancer, and there is no escort. When I was so thrust, I uncannily met my counterparts, Janice and Tom. Janice was a strong, determined woman who believed primarily in self. She did not believe in medicine and therefore put her entire well-being and treatment into her own hands. She rejected all medical intervention, and if she utilized anything greater than her self, it remained a secret liaison till the end. She was tenacious but died a painfully drawn-out death. Now, there isn't a doctor's visit I don't feel Janice over my shoulder. I understand her resistance more and more, for the things we're asked to do to preserve our well-being are not pleasant. Yet in the hard breath before each decision, I see her reliance solely on self and fear its imbalance.

Tom, on the other hand, was adrift. He seemed to have lost his sense of self and had a disinterested entropic view of the world. He put his fate completely in the judgment of medicine. And so,

I watched Tom grow smaller in the space he took up. I watched Tom give no resistance whatsoever to what doctors wanted to do. The English poet William Blake said, "Without contraries there is no progression." Tom presented no healthy contrary, and thus, there was no progression. He became invisible, vanishing piece by piece. By Christmas of that year, he no longer knew who I was. By February, he died.

I feel roughly blessed to have Tom and Janice as specters of where I must not go, though the further I travel here, the more compassion I have for how easily, in any given moment, the Tom in me or the Janice in me can take over.

While Tom and Janice died, I was broken and healed and broken again. The first time, my tumor vanished. It was a miracle. When its sister began to thicken the rib in my back, I began with fervor the same rigorous visualizations and meditations and intensive prayers for hours each day, desperate to enlist the same overwhelming grace. But after six weeks, I was exhausted and humbled, for the tumor in my rib had only grown. I thought I had failed. The fear returned, now as terror. And in making my decision to have that rib removed, I heard Janice spurn my doctor and saw Tom with indifference bow. But I believe in God and in this strange familiar terrain, known as me, in which life and He meet. So, I waited till these elements merged, way down beneath my understanding, and there, in what felt like calm balance, I said yes, help me. With that, it became clear that this time, the *surgery* was the miracle.

Once home, it hurt so much to breathe that it took several tries to make it to my rocker where I moaned and thought, *the part has no peace unless it can feel its place in the larger Whole.* I struggled in my pain of breathing not to become the pain in my breathing. I tried to focus on birds and light and the sway of trees. I petted my golden retriever while inhaling—anything to soften the cut of my missing rib.

7

Within weeks I had my first chemo treatment, which was horrific, vomiting for twenty-four hours, my missing rib lancing me with every heave. For the next three weeks I vowed I would not continue, would never open my arm to that needle again. But in the dark center of my pain, an unwavering voice said: "Poor, challenged man—the *treatment* is the miracle." And so, with more terror than I have ever known, I said yes and opened my arms to measured poisons. Finally, after four months of treatment, I sat in our wellness group where truth could relax its way out of hiding, and there I was asked to draw my cancer and my treatment, and suddenly I knew—the cancer was gone. Now the treatment was killing me, and the miracle appeared as the silent certainty with which I took my good doctor's hand and said: "No, it's over. I won't do this anymore."

What a revelation—who would have guessed—that miracle is a process and not an event and that each situation demands a different aspect of miracle: visualizations, yes; craniotomy, no; visualizations, no; thoracic surgery, yes; chemo-cleansing, if I must; chemo-poison, no. And underneath it all: willful, constant prayer, an unrehearsed dialogue with God, as Martin Büber puts it.

Still, even years later, I am not exempt from the fear and fragility. We're always asked to enlarge our sense of things in order to right-size the fear and to carry our fragility. It's a constant challenge to find the current of life and to trust it, to behold the depth of what-is until a relaxation of intent and anxiety allows us to find the spaces in our individuality that we then know as Spirit. Only through the passageways of Spirit can we be lifted when we're heavy and rinsed of the exaggerations of our fear.

~ ~ ~

During my odyssey with cancer, I learned a great many things. One of the most crucial was the almost simultaneous need to inhabit myself while staying connected to others. With each test, office visit, surgery, and treatment, I had to prepare, as best I could, for things no one could anticipate. In order to do this, I had to center myself and connect with the underlying flow of Universe that fills me with a strength and perspective beyond my tiny self. To do this, I needed to be alone. I needed to enter my solitude, which once entered becomes a threshold to everything that is elemental, eternal, and divine. All my loved ones grew to expect my gathering inward, especially before each medical procedure. But once centered, once in the Universal flow, I had to connect with my loved ones in order to endure the experience.

Now that I'm well, the ways in which we survived—alone and together—have stayed with me, and the more I have thought about them, the more they represent a basic and unavoidable paradox about living, which is this: Though each of us must go through our suffering alone, no one can make it alone. Though no one can save us from our own feelings, not one of us can carry those feelings in the world without the support of others.

I remember wheeling Ann to her surgery, her stretcher wobbling down the sanitized hall, her groggy eyes looking back at me, our hands entwined. I wheeled her as far as they would let me, and then, quite suddenly, though I knew it was coming, the glass doors of the operating room stopped me and she was wheeled on. I stood there, pressed against the glass, watching her grow smaller and smaller.

I realized then that whether it be our search for purpose, our struggle with confusion, our working through grief, or the violent evolution of our identity, no one can go beyond the glass door with you. Each of us must do that work alone. Each of us must ask our questions and feel our pain and be surprised by wonder in the very personal terrain that exists beyond that glass door. The best we can do in loving others is wheel each other as far as possible and be there when our loved ones return. But the work that changes our very lives, the work that yields inner transformation, the work that allows us to be reborn within the same skin must always be done alone. This is the work of solitude, and the attending to and from the glass door is the work of compassion, and the sharing of what we each discover in our solitude is the work of education, and the wisdom by which we weave that inner knowledge and that compassion—this is the work of community.

Whether walking a loved one into surgery or investigating the spiritual formation of teachers, we need both solitude and community to enliven our compassion. For only both paths—inner and outer—can yield the miracle of the Whole.

Yet how do we access the flow and miracle of the Whole? How can we when broken, open ourselves to all that is not broken? It all begins with faith—faith in everything larger than the singular self. It helps here to remember that faith is inextricably linked to care.

As the theologian Paul Tillich contends:

> Faith is the state of being ultimately concerned, an act of the total personality. It is the most centered act of the human mind.

Ultimately, faith is no more than the willingness and bravery to be ultimately concerned, fueling that fire of concern with everything that matters. The mystery is that taking the risk to be so ultimately concerned *in itself* makes us more whole. And what is compassion, but being ultimately concerned about something other than ourselves?

In actuality, miracle is the process of ultimate concern, and one aspect of miracle is what happens when love makes us cross over into the sharing of each other's pain.

~ ~ ~

So here I am, like you: not healed, but healing; not sure, but gaining in confidence; no longer a bother to others, but still troubled; full of wonder when not in pain. Here I am, thrilled and raw at the prospect of waking one more time. I stand before you, humbled, a Lazarus of sorts, and I don't pretend to know half of what has happened to me.

What I do know is that cancer in its acuteness pierced me into open living, and I've been working ever since to sanctify that open port without crisis as its trigger. But can this be done without crisis pushing us off the ledge? That's the question now, years from the leap: how to keep leaping from a desire to be real so as not to be shoved by an ever-lurking crisis.

Oh how do I give you where I've been? How do I open my palms and say, see how pain has simplified the air, see how struggle has boiled down to joy? They say that birds dream in the nest and whatever they see makes them wake and sing. How late must it be for me to whisper that our nest is our suffering? How quiet for me to offer that living is in the vastness that experience opens. How utterly rearranged must we be to realize that loving is the courage to hold each other as we break and worship what unfolds.

WILLFULNESS
(For Nur)

To inhale
enough of the world
when you're told
you have cancer
so the dark fruit
never seems larger
than your orbit.

To do what you
have never done
to stay in the
current of life.

To fly 1,000 miles
to meet someone
you dreamt
might help.

To pray in tongues
you've dismissed.

To think in ways
others distrust.

To use money
like a shovel
to dig
for time.

To cross
the grasslands
between us with
a tongue like
a machete
cleanly
sweeping
a path.

To weep
when the pain
won't stop.

To breathe slowly
when the weeping
won't stop.

To insist
that friends
don't pamper you
or look at you
as sentenced
or contagious.

To slap the thought
from their eyes
with your heart.

To climb the days
like mountains
for moments
like summits

where the light
spreads your face
and the constant
wind makes you forget
the pains in
getting there.

To stand as tall
as the weight
you are bearing
will allow.

To rely
on your spirit
which waits within
like a thoroughbred
for the heel
of your will
in its ribs.

To feel
the vastness
of night
and know
you still
have love
to fill it.

To accept
you can snuff
in a gust, but
to stay devoted
to the art
of flicker.

In Voices Half as Loud

The MRI bounced its waves across my skull
and there, below, like some magnetized pond,
cerebral fluid pressing on my brain,
the bone worn through. Craniotomy was
on order. I was admitted and pumped with
Dilantan to prevent seizures and the injection
well was slipped in a vein on my right forearm,
#18, taped and initialed. And the anesthetist
came to interview: Had I ever been under? Was I
mildly or moderately aware? Would I call myself
nervous? She said, "Don't be alarmed if you
wake with a tube down your throat.
It's there to help you breathe."

My family came great distances,
unsure what to say. I felt well, alive,
afraid this liturgy would pour the spirit
off my brain. I had dreams of my surgeon
tipping my agitated head like an immature
coconut; he breathing gingerly through his
mask; me hovering above the swollen canister
that was me. The kind Irish nurse came on her
day off to show my wife where I'd wake, where
they'd stir me to make *sure* I would wake and
dilate and squeeze their well-trained fingers.

We began to pray for a miracle. What had I done?
What could we do? We prayed for a miracle.
To her God, to my God, to anything

more commanding than we. Dear friends
gave us crystals, highly polished with
their care. And another, a petal from Lipa
in the Philippines where Mary once appeared.
They say she loved the air till it rained petals,
hours of red from the sky. The petal, in a locket,
in a soft gold purse. And we prayed for a miracle,
not knowing how to ask. Over and over, till the face
on our heart stretched in pain. Give us a miracle
and we shall speak of it when the winters are too
cold for anyone to care. Give us a safe inexplicable
way to drink again from the ordinary days. My head
was shampooed and I was told to let nothing
pass my lips. Everyone said good-bye
and rushed to pick up things that
weren't there. The day went gray
and those who love me envisioned
the side they alone can see.

At four, our surgeon, face safe as a globe.
They pulled the IV. It bled for a while.
There was one more test. The bleeding stopped.
One more specialist. He was out of town.
They sent us home. I walked right out.
We ate with friends and slept at home
and woke to familiar noises
in the trees. We prayed every night.
I continued to feel well, whole, unaffected,
confused. The tests were mounting: X-ray, ultrasound,
CAT scan, MRI, bone marrow, tubes and tubes of blood,
an angiogram where they snaked the magic thread

into my brain, coaxing me to hold still,
despite the heat, hold still. A week
went by, and back in, laid out as if sleeping
while a bearded man slid needles in my head, a style
he learned in Sweden, three times, four times, and
shakily, he squirted, smeared and dunked the fluid
from my mind. That night we prayed, the flower
from Lipa on my heart, then on my head. To my God.
To her God. Whatever it will be. Let us heal.
The next day, an open biopsy while awake, peering
at the anesthetist, sitting on her stool with her
plastic valves, asking, "How do you feel?" Beneath
the sterile drapes, "How do you feel?" Their steps
were so soft. What did I feel? What odorless colors
were vapors from my head? I was sent home
with a flowered cap to gauze up my stitches.

The operation has been cancelled. I tell you
I feel fine. They tell me it is cancer and tomorrow
I begin six weeks of radiation, glancing blows,
five burns a week. The side effects, they say,
are trivial: a sunburn in the ear, along
the roof of mouth, a dizzy sensation perhaps
like losing one's grip. Will it stop me from
hearing as I reach? "You have no choice,"
the oncologist says, "the *treatment*
is the miracle. Without it—Lord!
The house would fall." He's seen it all,
"You're with us now for life." He holds me
up, "There's months of chemo and checkups
and blood tests down the line."

Why can't I forge a faith other than through pain?
We change the dressing now each night. Oh why
do roots burn in our Gethsemane?

Tonight, in voices half as loud,
we think of God as another day
and like the Jews spit out into the desert,
we hope we can *endure* the miracle
as we suffer what we pray.

TU FU'S REAPPEARANCE

The great Chinese poet Tu Fu (712–770)
has appeared to me in dreams
as a guide.

Out of the yellow mist
he came again, his Asian beard
in tow. We were on a healthy shore
and he sat cross-legged in the sand,
scratching delicately with a branch,
his slender head down. I crouched
and put it to him, "How do I block
the fear?" He kept scratching the sand
as if he hadn't heard. I grew angry,
"How do I block the fear?!" He lifted
his head and shrugged,
branch waving above him,
"How does a tree
block the wind?"
With that, he
disappeared.

WITHOUT NOTICE

F aith is no longer a construct, but some vital tool as urgent as an oar in the ocean or a prayer in the modern world. The radiation therapist who cares but can't look us in the eye glances at his watch and tells us that whole-head radiation could erase my memory and render my salivary glands useless, which would mean no more taste and incessant dryness, a ropiness in the mouth. My memory and my mouth are my instruments. They are fingers to a pianist, knees to a quarterback. So what am I to do? Life is breaking me down. When waiting in the anteroom for surgery, we were all lined up, four or five of us, and one by one the masked angels of this medical underworld were hooking us up. Next to me was a young black woman, an innocent, inexperienced being terrified of the needle that would make her sleep. So terrified, she moaned before the needle touched her skin. How I felt her moan. But this was her karma. The needle wouldn't take, and they had to try four, five, six times until it settled in a vein. I lay there on my back, my last pouch of innocence torn. Who will suture that? I reached for her, but we were too far apart. She moaned again, and I thought: *What on Earth is my karma? What do I fear and need to relinquish so deeply that I am here? I have always needed closure, have always planned the days minutely in advance, but as we struggle, it's clear there will be no closure. There will never be closure again. It makes me wonder if there ever was closure or is it just a fabrication like time, a rope of mind which humans need to get by. Is lack of closure my needle which—because I fear it—must be thrust at me four, five, six times until it settles in my spirit's vein? Is this odyssey the shakedown of all my time-tried ways? I have believed in the sea and now, without notice, I am forced to let go of the dory and push out, out, out . . .*

THE WAITING ROOM

The eyes of animals in paintings surround us. Their stare makes me confess that in the beginning, I believed I saw something no one else had seen, and that feeling of being another Adam fueled my days and sense of worth. Like most, I ingrew my own version of things: lamenting my lack of brotherhood while secretly exalting that I alone could see.

In truth, I was starting to shed all this stuff, but it took getting cancer to shake me of my need to feel special. And sitting here in a waiting room at Columbia Presbyterian Hospital in a shipwrecked part of New York, staring straight into this old Hispanic woman's eyes, she into mine—I accept that we all seek the same peace of wonder, all wince from the same weight of knowing, though we each speak in a different voice.

Suddenly, but cumulatively, like the crest of a long building wave, I know that each being as it's born, inconceivable as it seems, *is* another Adam or Eve, each of us unique *and* common. Now I understand. It is not my separateness that makes me unique, but the depth of my first-hand experience. Clearly, as I look around, the most essential things I sense and feel, we all feel. I meet you there. I believe this acceptance is helping me stay alive.

This burdened majestic Hispanic grandmother fighting her tumor looks at me across the waiting room without a word on this sweltering day, the way an old Egyptian slave at one oar must have looked at his younger counterpart three oars down—no pretense, no manners, no needed phrases, but simply with a tired soul that will not look away which says, though this body is chained, these eyes are your eyes and they are forever free.

ENDGAME

Death pushed me to the edge.
Nowhere to back off. And
to the shame of my fears,
I danced with abandon
in his face. I never
danced as free.

And Death backed off,
the way dark backs off
a sudden burst of flame.
Now there's nothing left
but to keep dancing.

It is the way
I would have chosen
had I been born
three times
as brave.

QUESTIONS TO WALK WITH

- In your journal, describe what it means to you to enter your own life. How are you being asked to do this now? What is preventing you? What small step can you take to enter your life further?

- In conversation with a friend or loved one, discuss the different ways you've experienced being willful in your life. Which of these willful stances helped you grow, and which kept you from growing? How would you like to expand your sense of willfulness now?

- In your journal, tell the story of a time when you felt our common humanity. What opened this connection?

- In conversation with a friend or loved one, tell the story of an experience that opened your lens of perception, that widened and deepened your understanding of life. How has this changed the way you meet the days?

- In conversation with a friend or loved one, describe a fear that you're experiencing now and the hold it has over you. Explore the difference between feeling that you're in the fear and when you feel the fear is in you. In your journal, enter a conversation with this fear, beginning with the question, "What is it you want?"

- In conversation with a friend or loved one, describe a time when you relied too heavily on your own opinion and a time when you gave yourself away. What was the cost of each? What did each experience teach you? How can you apply these lessons to a difficult situation you're currently facing?

- In your journal, tell the story of a time when you held another when they were breaking and describe what unfolded because of your care.

A TERRIBLE KNOWLEDGE

The sighted fin only implies the wonder of the great fish pumping below, and the sighted star only implies the ocean of light flooding the Universe beyond the range of our eyes. In just this way, everything worth knowing is cloaked in paradox because everything substantial defies being revealed in its totality.

Most of us are thrust to one side of a paradox or the other by events, or the acuteness of our suffering, or by the incapacities of our character, which can't quite accept the abundance of mystery we're subject to by merely waking. But the one-sidedness of our experience never mitigates the beauty or power of the multifaceted Whole, and, though we seek to experience unity and to inhabit wholeness, being human, it's a momentary affair at best, like balancing sticks on a fence, or words of truth on a tongue, or pains on a precarious sense of faith.

Yet, despite our limitations, there is in everything, as Aldous Huxley suggests:

> a Divine Reality substantial to the world of things
> and lives and minds, (an) immanent and transcendent
> Ground of All Being—immemorial and universal.

Every culture understands this, and, though modern science has done much to discredit the notion, there is a common, numinous quality in everything. The Algonquin Indians call it *Manitou.* The Iroquois call it *Orenda,* and the Eskimo call that essence of Divine Reality *Innua.*

People who have not found their way to an embraceable sense of God often name this vastness of essence Truth. In this respect, God *is* Truth, the Truth inherent in everything as it is. Perhaps Truth is

25

the common, irreducible presence found in all things, that mixture of light and stillness that we repeatedly find wherever we go—in the worn edges of stones, in the fallen bark of trees, in the winded eyes of strangers, and in the sigh of an elderly mind suffering through to its tenderness.

The most enigmatic and crucial paradox we encounter as human beings is suffering, which is such because of our ability to feel. Forms of nature that don't feel, experience what we know as suffering as breaking, shedding, eroding, or decomposing. Yet who can say if other life forms can feel? If you can dismiss the possibility, it's the same blinded form of thinking that will allow you to dismiss another person's pain because you don't recognize it.

Yet it's also our ability to feel that enables us to experience wonder and bliss. This twin-edged capacity to feel is, in itself, a paradox, an aspect of God. Our ability to suffer *and* wonder is indicative of a larger presence that sustains the world with its cosmic heartbeat. Of course, our greatest challenge as human beings is to live in such a way that the wonder of feeling out-fuels the pain of breaking.

Not surprisingly, the aspect of feeling that has its hold on us dominates our view. As far back as 1750 BC, Enlil, the Babylonian deity of wind and storm, observes this in humans:

> Mens' spirits change like day and night;
> When hungry, they are like corpses;
> Filled, they count themselves equal to their god;
> When things go well, they prate of mounting to heaven,
> When in distress, they groan of descending to hell.

What is surprising is how for centuries we've been able to discount the other side of whatever we're experiencing, as if to acknowledge joy while we're suffering will make our suffering illegitimate, as if to acknowledge suffering while we're content will undermine our peace.

Like a salve misplaced in the ruins of history, acknowledging both sides of the paradox we call feeling is a healing restorative, because the Whole in its fullness is more empowering than any one aspect, no matter how pleasant or quarantined from sadness that aspect might be.

While we are rightfully preoccupied with whatever befalls or uplifts us, its opposite is happening somewhere else at the same time—not minimizing our experience but complementing it. For every moment of love, there is somewhere a corresponding moment of loneliness. For every birth of possibility, there is a corresponding remnant of life decomposing.

Our reaction to this is filled, understandably, with ambivalence, which is only a smaller form of paradox. At once, it's depressing, never to be free of the breaking that keeps forming the world and the suffering that afflicts its inhabitants. At the same time, it's humbling and mystifying that we're all exposed and enriched by such an inevitable process of feeling.

Our personal suffering is often intensified by our want to control life. And failing to be in control while believing in control makes us feel accountable for all that breaks along the way, and so, there is guilt. But where guilt is secreted by a controlling mind, compassion emanates from an accepting heart.

Compassion connects us to the suffering of others. It has a magic all its own. Guilt, in effect, is an intellectualization of compassion that twists into a peculiar kind of mental pain. Compassion, however, fuels those who share their suffering with reserves of energy in the form of love. More often than not, the compassionate are strengthened by the fullness of that Divine Ground of All Being that joining with another makes present.

There is no question that the experience of great breaking brings with it a terrible knowledge that is life altering. And whether that breaking comes about by accident, injustice, abuse, or disease, suddenly and irrevocably we become forever aware that out of nowhere a force can come at any time without warning to remove or damage whatever it is that we hold dear. The ever-present fragility of life is no longer a secret. The precarious fate of anything living is now and forever in question. And those of us who have experienced such know that, no matter the job or task, nothing else really matters now but the ramifications of this great fact.

How we make a home for this knowledge determines whether we live in terror or in awe, though nothing we can do or achieve will make us immune from realizations of either. Once in our consciousness, the terrible knowledge that life is as fragile as it is brilliant makes certainty an illusion. Our acceptance of this fact releases the urgency of living, and as the trauma of breaking subsides, the urgency of living remains, indelibly traced like an unseeable scar. Once feeling this deeply, the notion that each moment is unrepeatable and capable of being broken open at any time instills a sanctity about the simple graces of living that most awakened beings would envy. In truth, nothing else really matters.

It is no accident that those who survive being broken and who make a home for the terrible knowledge are, in turn, at the threshold of enlightened living. Often, in our one-sided logic, we try to theorize that suffering is a prerequisite to deep living. In truth, inhabiting *both* sides of *any* paradox is what engenders deep living. In the case of the paradox of feeling, the pain of breaking and the wonder of compassion are polarities that, once accepted and allowed to mix, yield a sense of Divine Reality in everything we encounter.

If you set out to suffer in order to find wonder, a tact that is inconceivable to anyone who has truly suffered, you will only experience pain. Breaking and wonder are by themselves unavoidable. It's how we allow for them to reside within us that unlocks the sanctities.

Likewise, if you seek to avoid breaking in the guise of preserving peace, you will never inhabit your feelings and will only sever yourself from any chance of experiencing wholeness or unity. For, as you can't see without eyes or hear without ears, you can't be whole without feelings.

There are many who subscribe to an emotional solipsism; believing that if a life breaks in the world and I don't hear it or see it, then the life and its breaking do not exist. This is simply denial of the grossest sort, no matter how well thought out or articulated. Ultimately, it doesn't protect the denier; just further isolates that person in a blindness that becomes irreversible the longer one stays there.

Because we live, there's no escaping breaking. Because we feel, there's no escaping suffering. Yet if we can endure the pain of breaking, depths we didn't imagine will be brought to light. If we can outlast the abrasions of eroding, we'll wear our inner beauties as a skin. If we can persevere through the rip of shedding, we'll live by new sensitivities. Yes, if we can accept the decomposition of old ways, we'll be reborn in the same life, unsure of how we got this far.

From the beginning, the key to renewal has been shedding, the casting off of old skin. In essence, shedding symbolizes self-transformation, self-initiated by a covenant to grow. Those who refuse such renewal may yet be forced to undergo transformation anyway as a result of being broken or eroded by the world. Very often, both occur at the same time; that is, we shed from within and are eroded from without. Often, the pain of breaking induces a life to shed its stubbornness.

It's interesting that the earliest peoples believed in something that we in our hive of manufacturing have forgotten—that immortality is attainable by shedding. The Dusuns of North Borneo have believed for centuries that when God finished creating the world He announced that: "Whoever is able to cast off his skin shall not die."

But what does this mean? Not that we can live forever, but that the way to stay closest to the pulse of life, the way to stay in the presence of that Divine Reality which informs everything is to be willing to change. Still, change what? To change whatever has ceased to function within us. To shed whatever we're carrying that's no longer alive. To cast off our dead skin. Why? Because dead skin can't feel. Dead eyes can't see. Dead ears can't hear. And, as we've said, without feeling there's no chance of wholeness, and wholeness remains our best chance to survive the pain of breaking.

Of course, for human beings, dead skin takes many forms, the most significant of which remain intangible but suffocating, such as a dead way of thinking, a dead way of seeing, a dead way of relating, a dead way of believing, or a dead way of experiencing.

Even so, we must be clear that shedding always has a pain of its own. There is no escaping the underside of feeling. I do not advocate pain, nor do I sacralize suffering. I simply acknowledge the reality of it all. As Buddha says: "All life is sorrowful." But life is much more as well.

It's like saying all time is dark, which is true, but all time is light as well. Is life one stream of darkness interspersed with days of light? Or is life one stream of light interspersed with nights of dark? Likewise, is life one long painful breaking interspersed with moments of wonder? Or is life one long miracle of feeling interspersed with moments of breaking? Obviously, there are times we feel it's one and times we're certain it's the other. Another paradox for us to integrate. For it is both and how we allow for both determines the personal alchemy of our hope and despair, our optimism and pessimism, our belief and doubt.

Indeed, all life is sorrowful, if we can't move our center of living off the pain of that terrible knowledge. For pain and uncertainty alone, as real as they are, are parts of the Whole, and their counterpoints, wonder and peace, are parts as well. Together they move us toward an experience of unity that lubricates the harshness of our pain, while the pain itself can't help but make the wonder and peace all the more precious.

Trying to inhabit the paradox of feeling, the Sufi poet Ghalib confesses to a friend:

> I do not fear (Life's) cruelty.
> But my friend, your heart
> which beats so proudly
> is the first thing She will take.

Living is not easy, and living openly is both wondrous and dangerous. There are many concerns peculiar to human beings that prevent us from shedding what's ceased to work, including fear, pride, nostalgia, a comfort in the familiar, and a want to please those we love. Often we give up our right to renewal to accommodate the anxiety of those around us.

The Melanesians of the New Hebrides contend that this is how we lost our immortality:

> At first men never died, but cast their skins like snakes
> and crabs, and came out with youth renewed. (But)
> after a time a woman, growing old, went to a stream
> to change her skin; according to some, she was *Ul-ta-*
> *marama, Change-Skin of the World.* She threw off her old
> skin in the water, and observed that as it floated it
> caught on a stick. Then she went home, where she had
> left her child. But the child refused to recognize her,

crying that its mother was an old woman, not like this young stranger. So to pacify the child she went after her cast skin and put it on. From that time humans ceased to cast their skins and died. [Sir James Frazer]

When we cease to shed what's dead in us in order to soothe the fear of others, we remain partial. When we cease to surface our most sensitive skin simply to avoid conflict with others, we lose our access to the eternal. When we assume truths we've already discarded just to placate the ignorance of others, we remain prisoners of that terrible knowledge.

We start out so innocent and fresh, knowing nothing of pain or breaking. We arrive with unblocked energy, all aglow. We begin as if washed in a golden bath, as if each soul is dropped in its body like water in a mouth, and then we embark, crystalline and barely ready. The Twi of West Africa believe it is the God named *Nyame* who bathes all souls before they are born.

But, whatever the name, we're born with a light that constantly looks for ways to shine forth, each of us the courier of an energy that wants only to join with its original ocean. And this energy can lead us to the wonder of feeling, if we don't shut it down or wall it in. Perhaps this is why, after all my own trials of breaking, after all my awkward attempts at shedding, after all my inevitable roundings from erosion, after all my own suffering, I feel that light is ultimately my home. Despite the terrible knowledge, I feel an inexplicable safety in a moment's solitude washed clean by unexpected light.

In a daily way, the light within merging with the light without—this is renewing, if we can shed what continues to accrue in between. Some would urge shedding to the point of eliminating the self. But, though our deepest experiences are moments of unity in which all distinctions between self and other are for the moment erased, we need a self to stay alive. And caring for that self, as it endures the agents that remove everything non-essential from us, we begin to survive the paradox of feeling. We begin to inhabit Truth, and through our experience of light—within and without—we're slowly empowered by that Divine Reality immanent in everything.

Living within ourselves within the Whole opens us to a humility of being. As Joseph Campbell so profoundly suggests:

> For those who have found the still point of Eternity, around which all—including themselves—revolves, everything is acceptable as it is; indeed, can be experienced as glorious and wonderful. The first duty of the individual, consequently, is simply to play his given role—as do the sun and moon, the various animal and plant species, the waters, the rocks, and the stars—without resistance, without fault; and then, if possible, so to order one's mind as to identify its consciousness with the inhabiting principle of the whole.

Even so, such a centered way is not void of pain or frustration or sorrow. But when centered, the difficult things are ground in the crucible that is us, rather than we being ground in the crucible that is them, the latter being misery. When in misery, the terrible knowledge is all consuming, causing us to see the world through accusation and blame in an attempt to hold others accountable for the terrible fragility of life. When that fails, it causes us to see the world through guilt and shame in an attempt to blame ourselves for our suffering. And though we're certainly responsible for our individual actions and though people often hurt one another, no amount of good will or virtue will eliminate the pain of breaking that arises from the nature of living.

Indeed, when in misery, when consumed by the terrible knowledge, we empower the two chief reasons to fear death. The first, the fear of not being, is inevitable. But the second is the insidious nature of regret, the fear that we have not lived well. And thus, the prospect of not being is doubly empowered by the threat that all we have not done, all we have let slide or done poorly, all we have not dared to say will *not* be given tomorrow to rectify. Therefore, living a full life is the best way to shrink the fear of death. The less regret we engender, the more accepting we become of what is and what will be.

So how do we live fully? How do we withstand and inhabit the paradox of feeling? How do we endure the terrible knowledge that life is fragile and uncertain and still experience the immanent Ground of All Being?

I'm not sure. I'm only trying myself, each of us a tiny will striving to find and ride the Universal current without perishing. But faith seems crucial: the ability to stay connected to the Whole, to know, even when in the dark center of our pain, that somewhere there is joy and wonder. This is a hard bit of consciousness to ask for.

Yet, even failing, faith is possible. For even when suffering, the Whole goes on. And faith can be as simple and difficult as believing in the Ground of All Being when it's too painful to see. Hard as it is to accept, especially when hurting, it's the magic of acceptance that softens our pain. Such acceptance opens us to surrender. Such acceptance enlarges our view. By daring to feel what's before us, we begin to drift like a broken boat and the sea of all there is begins to carry us.

Ultimately, each of us is born bathed in being and loosed into the world, into the paradox of feeling, to make our way; breaking and shedding, suffering and accepting; each of us like the mythic *chien* of China, an enormously colorful bird that has only one eye and one wing. Into the paradox we fall, needing to find each other in order to fly.

OCTOBER STORM

When the most important things in our life happen
we quite often don't know, at the moment, what is going on.
C. S. LEWIS

We wake to an enormous rapping at the side of our house and there, the towering cottonwood whose milk pods dust our path in summer is almost with broken back in supplication to the wind and weight of twelve inches of snow. We have no power. No light. No heat. A symbolism for us we can't brook for long. No power. No light. No heat. The entire region. Over 170,000 homes. They're talking days.

Not only are we recovering from the latest medical lap, but all our favorite trees lie slain, across the watery snow. We lost our shadblow, those delicate three-day-a-year blossoms. All we can hear is the painful endless creaking of limbs that took thirty or forty years to ring and grow so that on May first or second or third, with ineffable precision each and every year, a beautiful little net of white could welcome us to spring.

No power. And still we pray, more like John Donne today, with more demand and fury than humility and repose—God, why the shadblow?! This never would have happened except the leaves were still turning, holding on for a week or two. They held firm and kept the snow. They wouldn't let go and down they came. The early storm caught them turning. Had they let go, like every other winter, the bare essential stalks would have slipped the wind. What costly lessons of the age.

How do I become lean and leafless in the midst of surgeons and oncologists? How do I let my illness go like a leaf from my body before the storm? I must let go, the last leap of faith, must give myself over, must not be caught turning brilliant, must not go down with the storm. I must not cling to old inner leaves, old fears, old dreams. I must not break like autumn trees. A brilliant break is still a break.

So, in a world were men go long hard years to school to become cosmetic surgeons, surgeons of appearance, in a world where people pay them to rearrange their features so they can never face who they are; in such a world, my last moat before wholeness is to give up all appearance, no matter how thin what remains.

My last leap is in that river of light that is God's and mine, in that purity of life-force that makes these sore hips dance till the dance relieves the soreness, in that purity of being that makes my sore head swim through the sea of uncertainty till what's outlived us all begins to ease my frightened mind.

The day the trees fell. We're out trudging in the midst of sixty-degree sunshine, brilliant accent on the wreckage: orange maples split at the trunk, long slim elms reaching for the sky snapped in frozen gesture, and stubborn oaks wishboned and standing. The day the trees fell. As I await word about another biopsy, Ann refuses to let us be driven from our home. Home, she says, is greater than the storm. She boils soup on the Kerosun and puts candles by our heads. And as she rocks my fearful being in her arms, I begin to strip the excess that remains.

POST-OP

I could see it in your eye
when you thought I was dozing.
You thought you might lose me
and you started to remove yourself
as we do when pets are about to die
or old friends have decided to move.

But we are *living* with this,
not dying from it, and I
am not going, not until
the red bird flies
into the sun.

And you must not
corrupt the time we have
by double-living
what we will not.

So come on back.
Tell me your pain.
Utter your fear.
I feel it anyway.

This I've learned, the pain
makes the secrets known.

And so I saw you
sinking at the foot of my bed
watching the tubes run in

and out, saw you start
to fix the scene in your
future as a sad memory
of when I went away.

Come back to me. Now.
There are many futures
and each depends on us
today.

This is not about dying.
I have agreed to suffer
and therefore will live
like a gypsy exhausted
from his dance.

And you have chosen to love me.
So you will play my tambourine.
You will coax me to try
and urge me to stop.

And you will not have me
cleanly: in your life or not.

No. You will suffer too,
as I flare and fade
a hundred times,
while you marvel
at the secrets
I cough up from
the other side.

SETTING FIRES IN THE RAIN

You see. It was time. The tube had to come out. It had drained my lung of blood for days, through a slit in my side. The doctor was waiting, and I looked to Paul at the foot of my bed. Without a word, he knew. All the talk of life was now in the steps between us. He made his way past the curtain. Our arms locked, and he crossed over, no longer watching. He was *part* of the trauma and everything—the bedrail, the tube, my face, his face, the curve of blanket rubbing the tube, the doctor pulling the tube's length as I held onto Paul—everything pulsed. And since, I've learned, if you want to create anything—peace of mind, a child, a painting of running water, a simple tier of lilies—you must crossover and hold. You must sweep past the curtain, no matter how clear. You must drop all reservations like magazines in waiting rooms. You must swallow your heart, leap across and join.

THE DECISION
FOR THERAPY

As we gamble on the future,
let's stay clear: this moment
with all its presence is intact.
It is not up for grabs.

This moment for which I've
lived all others, for which
I've withstood the breakage
of all I know repeatedly,
this moment is germ-free
and not on trial.

You are welcome here
by permission only
and the alarm you cast
like a blind fisherman
will only snag my want
for tomorrow, only hook
what I do not have.

I know you mean to help
and I cannot deny
you are a bridge
I have to cross.

But where I live
cannot be staged
or stained or seen
as gross evidence.

Where I live
is impervious
to histology.

It is the one site
in the city that
will not burn.

And if you guide me
to tomorrow, I'll
show you, as you
shake your head,
how I still glow
in this unbreachable
clearing I carry within
like a sun or rising star
protected by its rays.

Questions to Walk With

- In your journal, describe your history with shedding your skin and letting go. What does letting go mean to you? In what ways are you being asked to let go now?

- In your journal, describe a time when you emotionally left an authentic situation too soon. What made you remove your presence? What might you do to stay present the next time you find yourself pulling away?

- In conversation with a friend or loved one, tell the story of someone you admire who stopped watching in order to join in the journey of another. Discuss why you admire this person and explore where this ability to lean into life lives in you.

- In conversation with a friend or loved one, describe a moment in which you felt the Divine Reality that exists in everything. What did that feel like? How did feeling the common aliveness in all things affect you? Where might you find such connection again?

- In your journal, describe a situation in which more than one thing feels true at the same time. How are you meeting this? What happens inside when you try to choose between truths? What happens inside when you try to open your heart to let both in?

- In your journal, describe a time when you put on an old way of being, thinking, or feeling to appease the fear, anger, or worry of a loved one. What did assuming a dead way do to you? What would happen if you discarded this old, dead way? What might happen if you try to be who you are everywhere?

OCEAN OF SKY

The cloud shelf drifts toward what
still seems possible and the trees throw
up their arms wanting to follow and the
Brazilian singer in the iPod is pleading with
me to give up all that drags my heart. Now
the sparrows out of nowhere dart in all
directions like the tail of a sparkler set
off in the beginning. And the singer a
continent away sings. I don't understand
a word but feel him like a brother, like
a voice wanting me to wake, like a secret
spilling from the lips of a forgotten god.
Oh, we've made it to another fall. The
wind swirls in and out of all my regrets.
We are alive. We are alive. We are alive.

FOR MY BROTHER

You were there when I had cancer
and now you've carried Dad over the
rickety bridge of his bones to whatever
time is left. And somehow you are tend-
ing the argument that is our mother
like a kettle without a handle.

For all your gifts, your care is the well
that has no bottom and, though hoisting
it up bucket by bucket turns you inside
out, that you know no other way
makes you my hero.

Covenant with Time

In silence or in crisis, we can put
down the gun, bandage the wound,
carry the water and share our bread.
But under all that, all we can do is
hold each other and listen. The one,
an indispensable lifting. The other,
an indispensable putting down. So
when you fall, I will help you up.
But when I fall on the inside, just
sit with me and rub the cuts no one
can see. This is how we make it to
tomorrow: fall and rub, lift and put
down. Like a piece of cliff letting
go after a thousand trials
to add to the shore.

AS RACHEL WAKES

I watch as you return from the tethered sleep of your surgery, and I realize that the things that fell us change, but we take turns, life after life; one of us bearing down to make it through while the other soothes and calms as we go. As you return, I feel our counterparts in the river of time—a Spanish seamstress cups water to her brother's lip, and a Greek sailor dips his captain's swollen leg in a stinging sea, and hundreds-turned-angel rock another's head or rig a splint or soak up someone's blood—and I step with them as I brush the hair from your tired face. You are back.

I see the needle in your arm and feel my lifetimes of puncture. You stir and ask, "Will you come again?" I'm going nowhere, sweet-innocent-wearing-down-to-love, nowhere but here, where I have landed over and over. Don't we all live like this, trying to bear what weighs us down? Isn't this our unspoken bond: to lift what will crush us, hoping when we tire someone with fresh legs will spell us for a while?

Your will to live ripples beneath your pain, and I know that God in his kingdom of blinding light sparked us to be spirit-moths drawn to what refuses to die. So we hover when the other breaks. I don't know why there is this geography between pain and peace. Or why we need to be broken for the element of love to take over. Or how many lifetimes we must suffer to understand that we do this in order that the Universe can complete itself. How many times must we trade places to wear a path between us?

While you were under, the peonies opened. It is their small pushing through that enables me to believe. We may never speak of this, but I have seen the very seed of what has lived forever. All this I saw in your small thirst upon waking.

Dance of the Seed

The beauty of souls laid bare is that we are then
all naked at once, together, our sameness and our
differences revealed in the glory of the truth of us.

B. NUR CHEYENNE

On March tenth, near three in the morning, Bob, sleeping in a lounge chair beside his daughter's bed, was awakened. The room was quiet, but something had changed. Nur's breathing had slowed. Her face seemed to be fading. He gathered the family and, once assembled, as if she were waiting, she let go a small and peaceful sigh, and was gone.

I first met Nur three years ago when I joined a wellness group, a small band of cancer patients traveling in this lifeboat we agreed upon, a lifeboat of an hour and a half a week where we pulled each other on board from this dark ocean we were drifting in and briefly held. I had just received my first chemo treatment, which was horrific and botched. I was traumatized and terrified to continue, terrified to stop.

But this is about Nur. She had cancer, and somehow she found extraordinary courage without minimizing the deep plethora of human mood that was her. She lived fully and longer than anyone ever expected. Still, that doesn't say enough, doesn't address the lesson of Nur, the gift of Nur, the ache that is her absence.

For one of those years, she wheelchaired to two of my classes and changed the lives of my students simply by being present, never focusing on herself, never hiding the struggle she was waging. She had a thousand things she wanted to do and, in spite of a dark underlining which was always much too critical of her

48

own limitations, she continued to work, to be a single mother to two sons, continued to write her poems, and take her chemo. We all grew accustomed to her routines of survival and looked on in mute awe as she would inject herself with treatment after treatment while talking from her heart, fully engaged in another's moment of fear or frustration.

During this last year, there were times she began to feel herself pulling away from the mainstream of life. She resented it. And though her parents were devoted to keeping her mobile, she began to envy the things non-cancer people take for granted, like walking to the mailbox, and chewing large overflowing sandwiches, and going to the movies. But through the full disclosure and animation of whatever was rising through her spirit, Nur kept returning to a center that seemed a bit calmer for each journey there, a bit brighter for each stumble into darkness.

In truth, her eyes seemed to shine brighter as her body shrank. Being in her presence was like nearing an intense light whose field of warmth would radiate into our emptiness. The more she struggled to stay alive, the more she bathed us all with this intense and Universal light. Soon, her battered, tired body seemed a buoy, marking where she was diving into waters humans still alive can rarely go, and then she'd surface saturated with this light which would pour from her eyes. At times, it seemed those incandescent eyes were holding her up.

We helped each other stay alive. We let each other cry and rage, and urged each other to go where no one else could go—into the heart of our own survival. The lifeboat had its fire by which we kept each other warm and, as is inevitable in such touchings, no one could really discern who the fire belonged to; though we are certain each put a piece of him or herself in to keep that fire going.

 ~ ~ ~

Today, the birds woke me, more beautiful for your passing. Where are you, Nur? All week I've felt empty and alive, useless and fingered like dirt. All week I've heard you whisper behind piano music, unlacing my heart. We're more for knowing you and less for losing you. How can this be—more and less at once? Amber says, in your last lucid moment with her, you dismissed the morphine, acknowledging it erased the pain, but lamenting the loss of feeling, knowing without the feeling, however bad, you must be nearing death.

Saturday, Paul and I walked the north field letting Saba run without her leash. The sun came out as we talked about you and death. I was telling him that I've finally, humbly, given everything over to love. No want for any possession, no secret dream, no fantasy of power or desire—nothing now beyond being split and stripped as kindling for love. Anything to keep the fire going. I was telling him how I would have done anything for you, how I will do anything for those I love, anything. The sun turned brilliant. My emptiness returned, and I realized, after offering everything, that while there's much we can give another, there's really nothing we can do for each other. No pain can be carried for another. Each is a felled tree we must lift ourselves. No lack of esteem can be lanced and healed for another. Each is the puncture of a nail we must remove ourselves. No blanket of hesitation can be pulled back from another. Each is an accidental hood we must shake off ourselves. The sun turned brilliant, and it made me accept—give what we will—there is nothing but bearing witness with a soft hand. So we walked, feeling empty and alive, and my dog ran in the light, and we walked, feeling everything at once, wanting to offer it up, knowing it would not alter the course of a life, the events of a death, the course of anyone's life but our own, which, no matter how individual, will pool in the mysterious vortex of everyone's death, everyone's life.

And as we walked, feeling like trees growing toward the sun, though these roots we call legs are never still enough to root, Saba began to poke at something to our left, poke and growl, approach and back off, circle and paw, dart and leave. She flipped it over. It was a sheep's skull, teeth up, sockets in the grass. And instantly, Nur, as if God had tossed this figure from His alphabet of metaphor right in our path, I knew this is what I've been doing with your death.

Just sniff, probe, poke, and growl. We watched the primal dance, learning from
my dog. Until, with a simplicity hard won by humans, she trotted on, leaving
the skull totally behind, sniffing for the next moment, following the light, the
wind, the cascade of a fallen leaf.

But we are left with our consciousness. We poke the skull and circle back.
Today, I can't stop poking. Where are you, Nur?

~ ~ ~

Nur's death triggered me into old unhealthy behaviors. Without
realizing it, the smallest task became urgent. My Cinderella
thinking returned with its subliminal dictum: let this pass
and you will turn into nothing. But maybe this is just what I
need: to release all constructs, to be defined by *no thing*. Each
significant death to this point has made me reassess who I am
and what I'm doing. The shock of life's fragility has made me
change so as not to waste the thread of time I have. But after
my own illness, I *am* living fully, not wasting a moment, not
squandering a chance, not racing toward tomorrow or burrowing
in the past. Now, there is no overhaul necessary and no work, *no*
thing to divert me from the full impact of this loss. Now, there
is only the soft and unnerving challenge to simply feel the
emptiness and starkly *be*.

Nur was like a worn stone cast high above us and watching her,
helping her come back to us brought us all together. Yet as such a
stone enters the deep, rippling everywhere, the impact of her going
is sending us in all directions back into life. This is painful to accept.
Nur's dying kept us together, and her death is sending us apart.

Yet she is in us. We *are* her. She made sure of this, moment
after moment, month after month, warming us each time she
flared, and the heat of her spirit is now under our skin. If she
taught us anything, it is that though we part, we never scatter.

51

~ ~ ~

Within forty-eight hours the priest who laid hands on my tumor has died, and this remarkable woman, who fought for years against her disease beyond even God's expectation, has suddenly dropped to the other side, and our dearest friends, joyous in their newfound pregnancy, have lost their child.

How to make sense of such things, especially having been close to death myself. I wander aimlessly in a saddened shock, feeling powerless and grateful to be here at all.

Having almost died, I find myself so easily punctured with the soft cry of loss, though I accept the merciless, unpreventable fact of it. It's not a morose resignation I'm feeling but a deep acceptance of the fragility and wonder of how many things attempt to live and how few are granted without preference the chance to do so.

Father Steve, a hulk of a man with a voice that had the gravel of an ancient river, had wanted to touch so many with his heart, and here it broke on a street in Rochester, as if he tired from carrying more than that muscle could bear. And Nur had resurrected herself so many times, I truly believed—despite all I knew—that she would live forever. As she was going, my soul went limp, aching for the glory of this unrepeatable spirit not to fade like a sunset behind the cold mountains.

Then to learn that Adam and Denise, who believed that the presence growing inside her was their child, who spoke to this unnamed aliveness nightly as it began to form, who wondered with glee at who might be growing eyes and lips to meet them—to learn their child will not be.

By what miracle of chance are we watching and they suffering, are we here with our pain of loss and they gone, not to feel pain anymore? Why can't I cry? It cuts so deep. But no release. Pain without tears is a saw with no oil. Yet somewhere I know that to cry for someone who has died is to open the heart's loneliest chamber so that they, no longer in bodily form, can enter. These deeper tears are the work, and the wage is that the person gone then lives within us. They breathe when we breathe. They are the unexpected urge rising in our voice.

It seems life is a dance turned war turned dance: all of us on the front line, side by side, arms locked with those we hold dear, all of it beyond our control, never knowing if the sister to the left will be dropped by disease or if the strange friend who never complains behind us to the right will be driven insane. We're asked to feel it all: accepting this is nature's way, knowing it could be us, feeling the loss of those whose grip is suddenly not there, and treasuring all the more the lonely awesome fact of our own survival.

There is nothing more to do but step forward together—and, when necessary, alone. We never held anything back each time we were together. This is love. Father Steve taught the big rural farm men how to love. And Nur taught us how long a spirit can stay on Earth like a songbird inside an empty sack. And what might that little child forming have taught us.

Perhaps they'll meet on the other side. His heart. Her eyes. The child unformed. Perhaps they'll seed a woman who will seed a saint. They say children who die in the womb become God's smallest angels. I imagine them wingless and voiceless. God's tiniest minnows.

Years from now someone we don't yet know or a godchild grown will ask about the man with the huge and burly heart, will ask about the spirit that would not die, about the child that never arrived, and we will look at each other and try to say things no language can embrace. It might be a summer night and maybe, if the listener tries hard enough, the breeze more than our words

53

will move them for an instant to consider us in our passing, never knowing how the dance of seed, for all our cries, goes on and on.

It takes six million pollen grains to seed one peony, so tremendous the effort to live and so improbable the chance to blossom. Yet we are all such a field of possibilities; except each human grain has a spirit, a mind, a heart, a thicket of hope tight within its chest. This is what makes life such a remarkable trial, oppressive when our efforts don't take and miraculous when our heart comes alive; each of us never knowing till it happens whether we will seed or not. And yet, every day we are both.

A SACRED MEDITATION

B. Nur Cheyenne (1946–1991)

Being a guest,
I walk quietly
into all the rooms
you have prepared.

Full of unknowing
I tell my own story
of dragging the pain
shackled to fear.

Being a guest,
you offer me cleansing.
Washing gently, I lift away
layers of scales covering my eyes.

Silently opening,
the door before us offers
an entry into the Never-Seen.

Gently rocking
you suggest I awaken
from sleepless nights
into the moment of now.
Trusting you mostly,
grasping my flashlight
I peer into black velvet caves
that open to streams
which flow into oceans of skies

that cradle the stars
who radiate light forever.

Being a guest
my heart is expanding
my eyes are more-seeing
than when I force my way in.

Fear is still present
sitting beside me.
I ask it to wait before speaking
(it has nothing to say).

In this expansion
Life is more present.
It opens before me, a widening road.
Ever-branching, many choices,
its riches surround me.
Jewels shimmer within me.
I am a gem.

Being a guest,
Death is an Innkeeper.
The no-vacancy sign
lies unused in the shed.

Watching the lights in the Inn,
they beckon to travelers
when they are ready.

Being a gem,
I build my own dwelling
across the field.
Walking my choices,
Living my Heart,
I garden my flowers
and water my plants.

Being a gem,
Abundance is flowing.
I'm sharing tomatoes
with the Innkeeper's cook.

Being a being
I am grateful
for God within you,
within me, within those
bringing me blessings.
Lifting my eyes, I keep
expanding my vision

till all of my breath
is all there is.

QUESTIONS TO WALK WITH

- In your journal, describe your experience of being fragile and vulnerable. Compare your experience to something in nature. Now go to this piece of nature that mirrors your vulnerability and watch it, listen to it, be in conversation with it—learn from it.

- In conversation with a friend or loved one, tell the story of a time when you were moved by something you didn't understand. What part of you, other than your mind, can be moved and make sense of things? How can this inner resource be of help to you now?

- In your journal, describe someone who's loved you unconditionally. What did that look like? What did that feel like? What do you think enables that person to be so whole-hearted in their loving? Whether that person is alive or not, write a letter of gratitude, describing that person's unconditional love and how it's affected you. If the person is still alive, send the letter. If they are not, send the letter to someone else, to keep their story of love alive.

- In conversation with a friend or loved one, describe a moment of love, beauty, or suffering that you experienced with someone else. How does feeling the presence of another affect your own experience of love, beauty, or suffering? How would you describe and name such a moment of common feeling? When drifting in the river of such feeling, what tribe do you belong to?

- In conversation with a friend or loved one, describe how you experience the dance of the seed of aliveness, in which we are, at once, close to life and death. Just as we make air useful when we breathe, breathe in the enormity of this paradox and help each other apply this mystery to a very real situation you face today.

- In your journal, explore what it means to a guest on this Earth and to be full of unknowing.

MESSENGER SIGNS

I stumbled onto Avicenna's *Poem on Medicine,* the medieval practice manual used in medical schools for almost six hundred years. He remarks on conditions with unusual physical detail. I read them now, a thousand years later, as a citizen of modern oncology, and take them as symptoms of our alignment with the Whole.

Avicenna speaks of messenger signs of death: "Diminution in the opening of the eye, deviation of gaze, and fear of light." Our openness is our lifeline. When we begin to close, we turn blue. When we shut our eye or squint, we lose the courage that looking into things brings. When we fear the light, we're doomed. He speaks of fatal signs: "Groping of the hands about the pillow, and if, at the end of sleep, one sees himself covered with snow."

I fear these things, for I have groped my pillow, but refuse the snow, and none of it has stayed with me, though each has skirted my being in darker moments. I believe deeply that our openness can save us. For God and Nature *meet* in us, *flow* through us. And I fear that the cause of illness, spiritually, stems from lodging what's dark, from stopping that natural flow. When breaking from the Whole, I clog and weaken.

As it is, I crest and crash repeatedly. When crashing, the dark hold on my heart tightens—the specter of recurrence, the rise of death into my thinking, the anticipation that small sores will be called tumors, that sweating, though it's August, might be a symptom. And though I must allow it, feel it, let it pass through, I can't make a home for it. If I make a home for it, it will take over my life. That's how this works. The darkness bites and waits to see if I'll scratch a hole in which it can stake its claim and fester and spread; physically, emotionally, psychologically. It's a constant battle, a constant logroll—me standing on my woe—first one way, then the other. I must let the fears and sorrows through. To bar them will strangely give them power to overcome me. I can't keep them out—the fears—but can't let them hover. I must enter them, like a muddy stream, let them churn up my bottom and flow on through.

I think our will, when exhausted of its want to control events, brings the self in line with the currents of the Whole, and healing is the rejoining that takes place. And if, as the great Russian writer Solzhenitsyn suggests, a clear conscience is necessary to induce new growth, it's because the clarity of our character makes a clean funnel of the soul.

Avicenna also speaks of the messenger signs of healing: "When a balanced warmth appears; when the senses grow acute; when one's movements take on strength; if one is quiet after a sleep that dissipates his pain; if a regular respiration appears, neither rapid nor slow; if the pulse is not restrained but full; and when the breath of a patient is not burning." This all affirms how Spirit, if welcomed, can enlarge the self.

From this stark edge between life and death, I must allow the elements their flow. It's the only way to health. To do that, I must somehow sustain the courage to stay open, to embrace and let go, to internalize and cleanse, to let fear decompose within into peace.

WHERE WE ARE STRONG

To the right, the tyranny of rejection.
To the left, the tyranny of being accepted.
I've lost good time with these lovers. In the
middle, this slim corridor of beauty closer
to Source than surface. Though middle
doesn't mean holding back or cutting
off the pain or joy. Middle means staying
in the heart of it, where we are strong.
I admit it's a comfort to sleep with what
is false and stark to be slapped awake by
all that is true. I know this comfort and
this slap. What? It's hard to hear?
I've spent my life coming to you.
Come. I'll meet you in what matters.
Step closer to the heart of it where we
are strong. We can walk and talk a while.

AS IF TO SAY

After his fourth stroke, he's given up
trying to speak. For the first time, he
doesn't know me. Like a worker trapped
in a mine, he looks up, as if I'm a stranger
happening on the scene. His eyes are wider
than one life can bear. I take his hand and
say, "I'm your son." He looks about as if
to say, "Am I still here?" I collapse into
a free fall, as the bird in my heart that
has followed his voice falls into the
canyon we both have bridged.

Later, he is back behind his eyes.
He grips my hand fiercely, looking
at me, knowing me, more deeply than
I can remember. In that moment, I am
certain: he understands everything. I've
wanted this depth between us my whole
life. He can no longer pull his fear up
around him, his body breaking away,
piece by piece. Wordlessly, we have
the conversation of a lifetime. He
won't let go of my hand or veer
his gaze. The TV across the hall is
blaring. The nurse drops a pan
in the hall. And my father on the
cliff before Eternity lies on his side
looking through me into the sun.

Finding a Way Out

When a dolphin leaps, something
in me comes out in the open. When
the truth in you breaks surface, some-
thing in me looks for a way out. When
I glimpse the vastness from a height, I
want to return to all I was born with.
It's true, breaking surface and glimps-
ing the vastness live in each of us. And
tripping through the days, we mirror
each other's sleeping angel. So when
moved way inside, open your heart
the way you would a bag of fire.
The world is a spark between
birth and death.

Questions to Walk With

- Since our openness is our lifeline, attend your own struggle, right now, and journal in detail about where your eye is closing, where your gaze is looking away, and where you find yourself fearful of the light. How can you course correct in each of these understandable exhaustions?

- In conversation with a friend or loved one, describe the evidence and rhythm of your own health returning to you. When do you notice a balanced warmth appearing in your heart? When do you notice your senses growing more acute? When do you notice your own movements growing stronger? When do you begin to feel quiet and peaceful after a moment of pain?

- In your journal, describe your history of feeling the tyranny of rejection, what being rejected has done to you, and the tyranny of acceptance, what you've done in order to be accepted. How do these experiences affect how you take risks?

- In conversation with a friend or loved one, describe a time when you could hold your heart open to the truth of what someone else was going through, regardless of how they treated you. Then discuss the challenge in being compassionate to yourself and to others at the same time.

- In the poem "Finding a Way Out" there is the line: "And tripping through the days, we mirror each other's sleeping angel." In your journal, explore what this means to you and, if you can, describe a personal example of such a moment. When the time feels right, discuss this with a friend.

- In your journal, tell the story of someone who models healthy endurance. What are three traits they demonstrate about endurance that you would like to be more skillful at?

Approaching Wholeness

The time that my journey takes is long and the way of it (is) long. It is the most distant course that comes nearest to thyself, and that training is the most intricate which leads to utter simplicity. The traveler has to knock at every alien door to come to his own, and one has to wander through all the outer worlds to reach the innermost shrine at the end.

RABINDRANATH TAGORE

How much we taste of life depends on the integrity of our relationships. I've been blessed to have good friends. They've taught me that the heart of relationship is tested when life undoes us, when we're forced by love to step from the confines of what we know in order to hold each other in the rough sea where nothing makes sense. It's love that leads us closer to wholeness.

The truth is that once turned inside out by experience, we're opened to the life of others and challenged to enter the endless river of feeling. Those who think they can skip over life by never showing their insides take a different road. Wholeness demands opening up and feeling. With those who won't accept this, there is less and less to share.

If blessed, we're broken of our stubbornness and humbled to discover the larger Wholeness we're a part of. Even so, relationships have a natural course. Some blossom and die, as we connect and disconnect. We lean on each other, then back away. We think we can make it on our own, then need each other nakedly. It's all very humbling.

I've learned over and over through my breakdowns and rearrangements that everything I've longed for was already close at hand. I just needed to recognize it, befriend it, love it, and embrace it. This changed what I'd been taught about willfulness and control. Tenderly, I've learned to align with the forces around me and have stopped trying to defeat them. To defeat experience is like a fish trying to defeat the very river on which its life depends.

By facing our troubled waters, we're called to the timeless question, "Who will live your life?" And to our surprise, our beliefs are lost or burned or torn apart along the way, through no one's fault. And though we can get stuck in the occupation of blaming, the loss of our beliefs is a vital part of the journey; so we can start again, sometimes more than once; so we can learn who we are and who we're becoming—all to get closer to this thing called life.

Still, when turned inside out by life, Wholeness seems impossible to grasp and yet every meaningful experience returns us to the fact that there is no "there"—only "here." From the confines of our pain, fear, worry, or doubt, from the confines of our immediate problem that seems to have no way out, *we're challenged, again and again, to realize the mystical fact that the air of the sky is the air in our lungs, that the immense aliveness of the Universe is the impulse of joy waiting in our heart, and that the vastness of peace we dream of is quietly waiting like a seed of emptiness in the very pit of whatever darkness we're struggling to free ourselves from.*

When something is whole, it's complete in itself. Though being human, we can't experience wholeness all the time or be permanently complete. Ultimately, it's through relationship that we approach wholeness, again and again. Along the way, life wears us down to what matters from the outside, while love prompts us into the open from the inside. So, to approach wholeness means that we can inhabit the gifts we were born with, from time to time.

The pieces in this section are personal accounts of the rough and tender wonders of relationship, and the difficult yet inevitable process of being turned inside out, and the unexpected feelings of wholeness I've been touched by along the way. Most of these pieces were written in my forties and early fifties. In "Troubled Waters," I bear witness to my thirty-year relationship with my oldest friend, Robert, and how being split open by life has only brought us closer. In "Who Will Live Your Life?" I affirm the irrefutable truth that wisdom and wonder are only palpable through direct experience. And in "Chores," I discover how the very atom of resilience waits in the smallest task. If we can tend to whatever is before us with all our heart, each task holds the secret of life. The poems in this section explore where the seed of what matters really lives and how love, exhaustion, faithfulness to each other, and surrender can open that seed.

Troubled Waters

I *t is unfolding like the bonsai I have been watching for months, waiting for the one blossom to finally open . . .*

Yes, Robert is a man of pure yet troubled spirit, and we have journeyed far these thirty years, waiting and watching for each other to open into new beginnings we barely thought possible. It is more than friendship. For we've been forced to hold—onto each other, onto what matters, onto life—like spirits clutching in a fire so ancient and hot that our centers have molded to one grip.

The bonsai is an Australian Brush Cherry, about seven years old. It is only eight inches high and issues only one bud a year. This small flower begins to surface in April as the tiniest green swelling, a fresh nub amid slender leaves. The clay sages that live beneath the tree watch for it, too . . .

We were in grad school when we met, and Robert tells the story, how he saw God in my eyes, no mask or refracted speech, just raw, unharnessed energy. I knew him also as an immediate spirit, someone I wouldn't have to explain things to, someone who understood the wonder that was my open secret. Here was a compadre I would not have to convince of the world of Original Perception.

We came upon each other, a pair of transcenders, in Maslow's terms, who:

> seem somehow to recognize each other, and (who) come to almost instant intimacy and mutual understanding even upon first meeting.

I put the bonsai in the sun daily, for direct light hastens blooming, the way real dialogue opens the human shell . . .

But we were far from whole, each bearing his own fracture for surviving narcissistic parents and each sputtering and steaming at the need to be of this world. Both of us were addicts; internally addicted to the Absolute Nature of Things, and externally addicted to whatever could soothe our pain at living in the world. For Robert it was drinking. He is recovering. For me it was making. I am a make-aholic. He was driven to drink to flee a relentless sense of never measuring up, while I was driven to make and achieve to alleviate the oppressive nothingness of not being loved. But these are common maladies, which is why I bother to address them.

This year, after the initial swelling, the bud on the bonsai seemed to stall and stay that way for weeks . . .

In the 1400s, Kabir said:

> If you can't cross over alive,
> how can you cross when you're dead?

We came to this. At first by dark inches and then by cataclysmic leaps. We spent many evenings seeking the smallest gateway to the Supra-Mundane, running wildly in the night, using anything to pry the ordinary open.

There were many thrilling moments, including the warm spring afternoon he introduced me to the poetry of Pablo Neruda. We were sitting on a grassy hill at the edge of the university when he began to read the rhythms of a voice I'd never heard but always known. I took the book, which he had borrowed, and wouldn't let it go for over a year. In those days, we gathered in the name of poetry, not yet ready to throw away the costume of art and simply be in God, though Robert was always closer to simply being than me.

But always at the end of our triumphs, in the glow of our pirated moments of the Infinite, he would trudge up his driveway in the dark as I dropped him off, wait till I was out of sight, and slink back out to the nearest bar. Likewise, I would simmer my

71

way home and sit in the dark at my desk, as my wife slept, trying to capture where we'd been, scribbling furiously, making, making, making, as if the words could keep the threshold open a bit longer.

Once out of each other's sight, we were drinking and making. He would twist lit butts in tablecloths and want to eat lightning. I would pound coffee and write all night long. These were the most desperate times because we had no idea that we were desperate.

~ ~ ~

This year, the bonsai's one bud began to push against its stalled skin in late May. I misted it daily, and it quietly soaked up what little water landed on its taut skin, and very slowly, very minutely, it began to stretch . . .

It was late in May of '87 that we embarked on grand explorations that would forever crack our world and thrust us through that fault into living on the other side which, of course, turned out to be nothing more than the undressed version of a reality we had been moving through all along.

I was going for seventeen days to Rome and Florence, the final trip of making after working ten years on an epic poem called *Fire Without Witness*. Ironically, though I'd tried to go for years, I was only able to go when the book was finished. I asked Robert to join me, but he balked and wound up fishing for a week in Canada with all his high school drinking buddies. Neither of us could know we were saturating our addictive selves with adventures that would change everything and which we had to undertake alone.

Robert entered a nothingness darker than he'd ever known, sitting in a fishing shack in the woods, drinking whatever was handy, eating nothing, dreaming nothing, hating nothing; while I began to surface in the ruins of the Roman Forum as if waking from a ten-year binge of making. On his way home, driving the thruway, Robert lost feeling in his hands and feet. It was the beginning of neuropathy, nerve damage that affects the extremities of long-term alcoholics. As he drove the highway, feeling draining from his limbs, I was sitting on the Spanish Steps in Rome, a lump forming on my head that I was unaware of, while, also unknown to me, my former wife was being diagnosed across the Atlantic with cervical cancer.

When I returned, Ann and I tumbled into a gauntlet of crisis that lasted three years in which we both underwent surgeries for cancer. I have written extensively about this period. It is the canyon through which this book like a river flows. But what hasn't been brought to light is the path Robert and I shared along the way; the evolution of that grip forged in fire.

As Ann and I went through months of diagnosis and testing, discovering we had cancer at the same time, Robert was going through intensive detox, getting sober to his core. We were all naked, raw, fighting for our lives, and the costume of art became cumbersome and weighty.

On a hot September evening on the sixth floor of Albany Medical Center, I was lying flat so as not to bleed after an angiogram and Ann, just days from being bedridden from her hysterectomy, was weak, slouching in a lounge chair at the foot of my bed. I felt some pain, and she tried to raise herself but couldn't. Her stitches were pulling. I heard her moan, and as I reached for her, I started bleeding. The nurses came, and we both fell back, and Robert was there, arms outstretched between us, a warm washcloth on each of our brows, more centered than ever, calming us and soothing our minds.

When Ann dozed, he held my face and told me I was meant to go through this, that it would, in the end, be good for me, for all of us. I didn't want to accept what he was saying, but as I resisted, I knew underneath that we were falling through the crack of our illusions into the reality and wonder of a single breath. Neither of us knew how to meet the days without being broken, or how to strip willingly of all that doesn't work. And when we don't put down what doesn't work, life zeros in on falseness the way fire and ice find weak surfaces to break. As Robert wrote later, "What ransom or allegiance dare save us from our lives?"

~ ~ ~

About two years into his sobriety, my cancer had festered in a rib in my back, and after surgery to remove that rib, I was faced with months of chemo. Robert and Ann were always there in golden silhouette behind whatever nurse or doctor was putting in or drawing out. Like medieval illuminations, they stood vigil over my pain, and it became too familiar to be always prone, looking up into their worried, loving faces ringed by clouds or sun or the changing array of ceiling panels from the many rooms of treatment.

In my last treatment, when I was hairless and pale, my veins had gone stiff, resisting the needles. The very cords of my body were saying, "No more." The dearest nurse had tried four times, and none of my darkened limbs would receive the injection well. I was sweating way inside, could feel a distant uncontrollable terror starting up like a scream on horseback galloping for me, its voice honing in before it could be seen. Robert took my hand and began to rub my forearm as they tried again. This time it took, though it felt raw and prickly like a stinger left in its wound. They began to drip the chemicals, and I felt that this was purgatory, neither dead nor alive but perversely forced by a cornered choice to take in drops of poison to cleanse a sickness that was growing, though it couldn't be seen.

Ann rubbed my brow, trying to wipe the fear rising in my face, while Robert read Neruda and Blake. What a vision they were. If you could have been behind my eyes. They seemed a dimly lit

74

Rembrandt. Seen from the eyes of the dying, who the viewer never sees, they hovered, a portrait of two ministers of spirit cleansing the body of someone cut by a sword or crippled beneath a rusty plow. As he read the words, Ann's touch seemed to sign them to the part of me too frightened to hear. We made it through, and I will never forget what they have taught; that reaching in and touching the spot that hurts, if done with selfless love, can release the pain the way a dark branch can be gently shook to free it of all those steely crows.

Within days, I lost feeling in my hands and toes. Ironically, the chemo had started to eat at my nerves, leaving me with the numbness of my brother. We both now had neuropathy. This brought an end to the chemo. It was summer, and in the weeks that followed, Robert and I would pick at sandwiches in the sun on a bench in downtown Albany, letting the light warm our nerveless hands.

It was there that suddenly, beyond the crisis, he looked into my very core and said, "I have your cancer," and I realized he had cut all boundary between us, so great was his love. We gripped each other's weary hands, the ends tingling with a new aura of numbness, and I said, "And I'm an alcoholic."

~ ~ ~

Late in May, as my bonsai was beginning to stretch its bud, we celebrated Robert's fifth anniversary of sobriety, and both of us accepted that, indeed, in the ways that matter, we are only five . . .

I found an exact copy of an engraving by Rembrandt, done in Holland in the late 1800s. It's of an old man with new eyes, and he's reaching out of his frame, his open palm extending to the viewer, as if to suggest there are no viewers, only those who see anew and reach. In this there seems hidden wisdom, in finding the courage to reach beyond our frame—of mind, of pain, of ambition, of fear. I matted the old man with new eyes, wrapped him in brown paper, and took him and Robert to Montreal for the weekend. That night, overlooking the blue city, from a room on the twenty-seventh floor, watching pigeons circle the lit statues on the church facade below, he opened his gift, and without words we knew that somewhere in Rembrandt's private center, he, like Shakespeare, understood the heat of the human struggle to be.

The next morning, we were up early, eager to walk the botanical gardens where they have the largest bonsai collection in the world outside of Asia. We strolled toward the Chinese Temple Garden. It was a lush yet simple retreat from the streets. It encompassed acres, a place of renewal originally constructed in the 1600s in China and moved stone by stone to Montreal in 1990.

As we approached the massive gate, it was locked. I panicked; ready to demand entry after driving four hundred miles from another country to see this. Robert calmly, like an Asian sage himself, treated the situation as if it were a koan, a riddle to be entered until its very assumptions shifted. He began to walk the outer wall of the Garden, which seemed insurmountable. I was frustrated. He kept walking slowly along the high wall. But the Garden stretched for acres, and I wondered if we were going to walk its entire perimeter. The thought made me cranky. He kept strolling.

Suddenly, when we had walked farther than was originally in our view, the walls disappeared. In fact, the Garden itself had no walls save for the façade at its entrance. We simply walked through the open grass to a path that welcomed us. It seemed profound that what loomed as an impenetrable barrier, a locked threshold, was actually a symbolic gate. Already, in entering the Garden, my frame of mind had been tested. How many thresholds that seem blocked or barred or locked, only seem so from their initial viewing? How many opportunities for true living are actually barrier-free, if we can only look beyond where we're told not to go?

In fact, once inside the Garden, there were no doors at all, only doorways, and every threshold had been placed just so, in order to point up a particular aspect of the Garden that might otherwise go unnoticed. And through the waterfall, we could see the inner pond. Standing there, it seemed clear that beneath the cascade of our feelings lies the pool of everything that is eternal. And only on that shore is lasting relationship possible, not just with other pilgrims but with the Universe itself. So, we, with our numb hands and feet, a cancer survivor and a recovering alcoholic who pulled each other up from the moist nest of sickness that is so much a part of our modern world, we, who had come from another country to find the gate locked, we walked through the waterfall into the pool and began to live with new eyes.

~ ~ ~

Finally, by August, the one bud on my bonsai began to show signs of its blossom. Small white tendrils began to pop through its hooded sheath. When I watered it, drops clung to the white tendrils and I would watch them disperse into the bud where no one could see. The way the bud absorbed the water showed me the truth of understanding: how covered with a clearness from experience, that clarity disperses beneath our skin to coat everything. I showed the white beginnings to Robert.

Just as the one bud began to open, I went away for our annual week on the lake, and there was something karmic about the fact that I would not see the bud fully opened. I thought about delaying our vacation, but felt that this was as it was supposed to be. For the lesson seemed to be in the acceptance that certain forms of truth remain out of reach, though their onset is what we know as beauty. So I packed the van with books and clothes and groceries, watered the budding dwarf tree, and drove north . . .

The second night there I had a dream in which Robert came to tell me that his cousin's daughter had been diagnosed with leukemia. Robert was upset, distressed, and I offered to go with him, to talk to his cousin. They lived in a suburban home. It was early fall, and the air was crisp, the color in the yard just emerging. As we entered the house through the kitchen, the screen door slapped a familiar slap, though I couldn't quite locate where I'd heard it before. Robert's cousin was a fallen, stocky man, somewhat heavy, though it appeared he was quite strong physically. He was at the sink stirring a cup of coffee with a spoon, and the spoon hitting the side of the cup sounded like a metronome of doom, a small, incessant, pinging underneath all the feeling that no one acknowledged.

The young woman with leukemia was seated at the kitchen table, more concerned for her father than herself. Our eyes met, and she seemed wise beyond her years. I really wanted to spend my time with her. I could see that Robert was struggling in his own way with the unanswerable tragedy of such a young life being threatened. She was the one who needed our attention. Her father, though understandably sad, was being self-indulgent, pitying himself. I put my arm around the fallen, stocky man, more to divert him than to soothe him, while Robert went and held the young woman, who either didn't quite realize what having leukemia meant or realized more deeply than the rest of us how fragile our moment of living can be. I woke to the sway of morning pines on the lake, the early mist rising.

That morning we drove into town to shop at some factory outlets, hoping to be swimming in the lake with the afternoon sun. We stopped at a shirt outlet. The little shop was a converted room on the second floor in the front of the shirt factory itself. As our friends started sorting through piles of bargains, I drifted back into the factory looking for a phone. Everything darkened.

There were fewer windows. The path between machinery and workstations was white-lined and zigzagged further into the musty place where shirts begin. There were older men running odd-looking machines that stitched collars and young women sweating at large press-like units that steamed the uncut linens. Finally, I found an old wooden booth near what must have been the office. I closed myself in from the noise and dialed.

Robert was at work. I told him of my dream. He told me that Gene the Source had died in the night from cancer. Among those in recovery, he was a sage. Robert's voice had a puncture. His sail was flapping. For here was a lost kinship, a mate standing the same watch on the same deck, and suddenly a wave of storm hit them both, and when he wiped the water from his eyes, Gene was gone. It all happened quickly. This man who was sober for fourteen years, who now knew the cost of a moment's true peace, who treasured that peace—within five weeks, he had been diagnosed and perished. He seemed a living alchemy of us both: recovering, cancered, treasuring peace.

The day before Gene died, Robert saw him in the VA hospital, among the wandering legions who never seem to heal. He was on Demerol, spacey, half-dreaming, half-babbling, and Robert gave him a kiss on his forehead as he was being wheeled away.

That night Robert randomly read from Blake and Neruda and from the Old and New Testament. And now, while young women were sweating at their press units, while old men were squinting in the half-light at the stitches pumping up and down into empty collars, while Ann and our friends were rummaging through irregulars, I sat in the wooden phone booth at the end of the white-lined path, buffeted by the incessant noise of machinery as Robert began to tell me a story in the book of John . . .

. . . about a man who's been an invalid for thirty-eight years and how he comes repeatedly to the waters which must be entered when troubled in order to be healed. He tries and tries, but can't get into the water because everyone pushes him aside. Jesus comes upon him near the river and asks, "Do you want to be healed?" The man continues his complaints about being constantly pushed aside. Jesus asks him a second time, more quietly, but with something firm in his voice that breaks the poor man's complaint, "Do you want to be healed?" This time the broken man focuses on Jesus, looking at the calm water in his eyes, and with sudden understanding, the invalid answers with a resounding, "Yes!"

Jesus crouches beside him, his hands close to his legs but not touching them, and whispers like a ray of light, "Then lift your pallet and walk." And slowly, the man begins like a cripple who is skeptical. As he finds unknown strength in his legs, he starts to rise like a severe arthritic. But as he begins to stand under his own power, he feels spirit in his blood-filled thighs. And once erect, spirit and life are flowing through his limbs, through his unthinking legs, igniting his awareness. Jesus slips into the crowd, and the man, not knowing who he was, splashes through the waters to rejoice, already healed.

The story says a great deal about how we approach and resist reality. The first issue we face time and again is that of needing crisis, troubled waters, to be opened to the terrain of true health, when only being is necessary to be healed (just lift your pallet and walk). Too often, we're so wrapped in our illusions that we need crisis to open us.

The word *health* can be traced back to the Indo-European root *kailo*, which means *whole and uninjured*. This phrase is also the root of the Old English word *halig*, which means *sacred and holy*. Not surprisingly, there's an innate connection between wholeness, health, and what is sacred. At their deepest level, they are the same. In truth, this innate trinity is a state of living, not an arrived at state of mind. We are constantly healing, never fully healed. We are constantly approaching wholeness, and can never be completely whole. We are constantly working to be here and to recover wonder, and are never finished and holy like a museum relic. Often, it's this never-ending attempt to heal that saves us by cleansing the buildup of pain and illusion that comes from living in the world.

But the story of the invalid raises another concern that can only be addressed if we consider all the characters as parts of a single self. In this context, the Jesus-self asks the invalid-self, "Do you want to be healed?" The invalid-self complains that he can't make it to the healing waters because all the other parts of his self push him out of the way. What unfolds is an intra-psychic play within a single soul. The divine light within asks the chronically weary part of us, "Do you want to be whole?" The frail and crumbling self complains that all the other aspects of his self come first. The spirit in us asks the wounded in us, "Do you want to be whole?" But we put aside our deepest sensitivities in order to maintain the victim's thrill of emergency. Our inner voice asks our most confused and hidden self one more time, "Do you want to be whole?" But divided into suppressed parts, we hesitate and turn away, while the ounce of God's Being living in our center whispers firmly, "There are no contingencies, no bargaining-ifs, no need of troubled waters. If you want to be whole, simply lift your pallet and walk."

So lifting our pallet seems crucial to assembling the many parts within us into an integrated whole. What can this mean? The definitions of the word *pallet* seem to be voices in a song. The ancient definition is that of *a narrow, hard bed or straw-filled mattress,* which comes from the Latin, *palea,* meaning *chaff.* So lift up your chaff and walk. Discard your excess and be whole. Separate your husks from your seed and be. The evolution of definitions is also helpful. Pallet, *a portable platform for storing cargo.* Lift up your portable platform and begin to heal. Stop trying to take everything, material and not, with you. Give up trying to save and hoard everything you experience and become holy. Pallet, *a tool used in applying gold leaf.* Lift up your gilding tool and walk. Experience rather than name. Hold rather than value. Embrace rather than assess. Pallet, *a wooden potter's tool for shaping clay.* Lift up your shaping tool and allow yourself to be shaped. And so, the ancient voices sing: Stop interfering and let things mix as they will. Stop controlling and excluding. Be direct and walk among the living.

The parable from John acknowledges the inevitable role of crisis in our lives while hinting at the dormant power of being. The parable suggests that when in pain we isolate our frailest aspects from the light, which light alone will strengthen. And the obstacles to wholeness that we perpetuate consist of the chaff we wrap ourselves in, the baggage we insist on lugging around, the names we delude ourselves with, the very mind we try to control events with, and the civilized gestures with which we divert the direct energies of life.

Persistently, we're opened by crisis to discover the healing power of being that was living within us all along. In time, we're all opened and, if blessed, we're shaken from the thrill and comfort of our crisis . . .

. . . but Gene the Source is dead, an alcoholic done in by cancer, and there we were, surviving brothers, breathing heavily into anonymous phones—he at work over a desk full of papers, and me, in a noise-muffled wooden booth in the bowels of a shirt factory beyond the range of light. Gene the Source, gone, and in his wake, the fear that all survivors suppress—it could have been me.

~ ~ ~

Later that night I wore a new shirt to a restaurant on a river in the Adirondacks. The river had a bed of broken rocks, which made the water ribbon and foam in many directions, and as dusk thickened, the waxwings with their incredible speed and agility hovered, snapping up bugs in the fading light.

One rock toward the center of the current wouldn't let me go. Half of the water was hitting the rock and coming back on itself trying hopelessly to buck the current and go back where it came from, while half was flowing over the rock smoothly, creating a silent film that simply moved on. I watched closely. The water approached as one mass and split into these two functions: curling back on itself whitely and slipping over and on clearly. Then I realized—this is how it works in us. The part that needs crisis in order to be real hits what it encounters, curls back on itself, and tries through resistance to return where it began, while, at the same time, the part in us that needs only to be slips over clearly and on. Both within us, happening at once.

On this side of dying, Robert and I have taken turns being the foam and the clearness, the turbulence and the quietude. Don't we all carry both as we meet the days: part of us ready to stir up whitely at anything we meet, and our deeper self ready to come closer and glove what we experience clearly? Isn't he in his drinking and I in my making—aren't we, in those moods of imbalance, the foam stirring whitely back on itself at the cost of all else? Isn't it the white agitation alone that ruins a life, whatever form it takes?

Enduring our own agitation, we must ask ourselves: Do we look for things to be troubled? Do we seek out troubled waters? Do we want to be whole?

~ ~ ~

While away, the bonsai had fully bloomed, and its tiny white tendrils had burst and shed. When I returned, the skeleton of blossom hanging in mid-air seemed the anatomy of a star that had lost its power to hide in the day. And oddly, I feel like that, no longer capable of hiding in the light, conspicuous wherever I am . . .

The next day Robert and I jogged through rows of secluded pines, breathing in rhythms neither his nor mine, and sweating and panting, hands on his knees, he said to me, "If we could only inhabit our lives . . ." And two days later, I jogged with my dog up and down the hill near my home and found that running off the peak touched me so. I used to push all the way up, eyes to the road, step after step, just to make it to the top. But here, coming off the peak, seeing the wind brace the willows as I crested and eased on down—this released joy, not going up, but coming down. Who would have guessed? We have simply fallen beneath the surface of things.

KNOWING GOD

Oh lone crazed bird
singing in the night—

you sing with your whole body
while the rest of us sleep.

I go to close the window
when my wife touches my arm
and we listen.

You call out
like a saint robbed of words.

Are you blind and trapped
in a vision of sun?

Or do you simply see farther
than the rest of us?

Do you see the light coming?

Do you feel the beads of warmth
forming in the dark?

Oh what has stirred
that thing in you that sings?

Stir me now.
Sing me clean.

THE GARAGE

This took place while planning for Ann to have her hysterectomy.
She was doing her doctoral work in New York that summer
and was home only on weekends.

That first week away, I thought, with her life so pulled and splintered, I could at least keep our home in order. So often, when things become chaotic and complex, she involves herself in cleaning or fixing or refinishing. But here, there wasn't even time to affect such a sublimation when she needed it most.

I sought to surprise her and do something she has asked for years—clean the garage, which had become a quagmire of suburban refuse: tires to cars long gone, copper caps to nothing, buckets with split bottoms, unraveled wicker baskets, fluorescent lamps with no bulbs, cardboard boxes to appliances we can't even find, rusted hibachis, labelless wine, sandpaper worn smooth, and oh yes, dead mice floating in an open bottle of anti-freeze. It took fourteen hours, three trips to the dump and two to the Salvation Army. I was pleased. I had scaled the inept homeowner's Everest. The summit was sparse, swept, labeled, organized, symmetric, emitting a rational if sterile peace.

So that first Friday home, after taking her exams, after light wine and soft stories renewed our closeness, I showed her the garage, and she began to erupt and suppress, by turns, a semi-hysterical rage. My stomach knotted. I couldn't understand. I tried to explain. She tried to explain. She feared everything she'd ever saved was trashed. I assured her I had exercised conservative judgment. She asked about Paul and Ann's iron sculpture—I'd thrown it out. She asked about her parents' lawn chairs—I'd thrown them out.

She burst into momentary rage, "Someday, I'll clean out *your* belongings!"

I shot back, "How can you talk revenge?! I thought you'd be *pleased!*"

She sighed, "I know what you intended, and I *do* appreciate it." Then she held her head and walked to the window and broke down, "Can't you understand? I'm losing control over everything in my life. My health. My work. My schooling. My body. And now, I can't even control my home. Can't even have control over my past."

She began to weep uncontrollably.

I felt a gnawing, rising, tightening twist beneath my ribs. It was a burning mix of love and stupidity. I know her so well. How can such care and knowledge blunder, as if I'm always spilling some favorite dish all over her lap. Had she not had her powerless lens on, she would have been pleased.

We worked it through like resilient doves. Neither of us wanted to fight, least of all with each other. I took her to me gently and offered, "I am ready to be anything, anything that will make you feel the peace you deserve."

She held me close. The fear of being ill made her moods quick and fragile as a hummingbird. We quivered and held on and repaired.

That night, there was such a quelling safety in sleeping together. We relaxed for the first time in weeks, side by side, each body a wing to the thing between us that believes it can fly. And then to wake with night warmth about the neck and throat and chest, to have heads rubbing half-awake in old familiar ways. There is no joy, not even the rush of climax, as permeating as the deep habit of sleeping entangled with an old, old lover.

In the morning, we saw a goldfinch with its small brilliant chest flutter at our window, and Ann told me, her stare fixed on the patch of clearness where the finch had been, that they turn brownish in winter to match the trees and yellow in summer to fool the bees. She is so lovely; my mind cracks, letting out its heartened voice. What must a spirit do to fool disease?

We had fruit salad on the deck in the sun, and she stared at me in the same soft way I have been falling into her. She finally said in a tone that precedes emotion, "I couldn't imagine myself living with any other man." It was then we realized the robin had hatched her eggs in the maple. Two red twittering beaks jerked up and disappeared, making the most strident and unfinished of moans.

Thank God we didn't disturb the nest. Such a simple ingredient to mortality—do not disturb the nest. That's what the garage was all about. Do not disturb the nest. The watering of her flowers has become more symbolic by the day, as if I'm watering her insides, fussing over veins that lean and small organs that curl.

LIVING WITH
THE WOUND

There is a need to be specific
if we are to survive,
which requires being honest,
the way seeing requires
the eyes to stay open.

It means I can tell you
when you hurt me
and still count on your love.

It means being honest
with myself, knowing
the ugly things are not
always someone else's.

I've been thinking how
practical people cut the cord
to those who've broken hope,
the way breeders shoot horses
with broken legs, as if
there's nothing to be done.

Now I know they do this
for themselves, not wanting
to care for a horse that cannot run,
not wanting to sit with a friend
who can't find tomorrow, not wanting

to be saddled with anything
that will slow them down.

I used to think it bad timing.
When I was up, you were down.
When you were ready,
I was scared. But since
we've never given up on each other,
it's clear that drinking wonder
when we're sad is how we shed
the things we love about pain.

I have a right to joy
even when lonely,
even when in pain,
and you never need
to cover your wounds
when entering my house.

If your voice breaks, I'll be a cup.
If your heart sweats, I'll be a pillow
on which you'll chance to dream
that weeping is singing
through an instrument
that's hard to reach,
though it lands us like lightning
in the grasp of each other
where giving is a mirror
of all we cannot teach.

QUESTIONS TO WALK WITH

- In your journal, tell the story of a pain and how it rearranged you. What in you is different for having experienced this pain? Are you more whole for experiencing this pain? If so, how? If not, how is the experience of this pain keeping you from being whole?

- In your journal, describe a time when you became too entrenched in the occupation of blaming another. What did the energy of blame keep you from in yourself?

- In conversation with a friend or loved one, discuss what it means to live with a wound. What does it mean to you to face your feelings and not drown in them? Share a personal example of doing this well and an example of doing this poorly.

- This is an inquiry into long-term friendship. In your journal, tell the story of someone you've journeyed with over time and how your bond has changed through the years. Describe what holds the two of you together. Describe three things you'd still like to know about this person. Go to them and honor the bond you have, and ask them what it's like to be them. Then ask your questions.

- This is an inquiry into personal trust. In your journal, tell the story of someone you lost trust in and how this came to be. Try to be honest about your part in this. What have you learned about the nature of personal trust? Later, in conversation with a friend or loved one, discuss how you might repair this trust. If that no longer seems possible, discuss how you might establish trust more thoroughly in a new relationship, applying what you've painfully learned.

- In conversation with a friend or loved one, tell the story of something that's taken a long time to blossom within you.

MIND SWEATS

Thank you for holding me in the night.
At unexpected times, the silence seeps
in like water soaking through. When I
am well, this is exciting, a form of
waking naked in the world. But
last night, I felt dispensable.

As if life were a secret we didn't
know we were keeping, a whisper
tucked near the heart, like an envelope
with special instructions: open only
if death seems imminent.

As if to follow someone with more
confidence would make a difference,
when our grasp on life falls apart
and reassembles repeatedly
like the hold a throated river
has on its debris.

In my fright, I know I'm going to die.
Not now, not soon, but *know,* the
way seeing all those images on the
news, one finally catches in your
throat, and you *know* that some-
where it is real, somewhere
there is only air between
the camera and the pain.

Last night, there was only
air. And you held me
in the dark.

We huddle in our love
as in a tent on a shore
watching our fears roll in like surf—
building, crashing, thinning—
knowing the swimmer
who withstands the pounding
can make it past the breakers.

FIRST TREATMENT

We cried in the car last night.
I vowed never to give up, while Ann,
in a moment that made us feel eighty,
said, "If it gets too much, you can."

How much is enough?
How much scouring before the face
is worn of its features;
the mind, its beliefs?

How many times can a heart
be made over like the handle of a tool?

When I look into the eyes of those
who love me and not their fears,
when I wash my head and rinse
my fears, when I hear my God
in between my suffering,
I realize the gift
like a chisel or harp
is in my hand,
and that you give back
by making good use
of what you're given.

CRADLESONG
(for Jessica)

How do I explain chemotherapy
to a six-year-old up in my arms
before I shed my coat?

How do I tell her I can't
kiss her on the lips because
my white count is low, that
we must leave early because
Aunt Helen has a cold?

And when we go, she hides
in her room, face in the corner,
till I return and swallow her
in my arms—Damn it all—
I kiss her anyway
again and again.

And next time, she's on my lap
staring in my eyes as if to see—
is there laughter behind them
or is that puppy on a leash, too?

She searches my face, then says,
"You're losing your hair."

I act surprised, "Where? Show me."
She runs her hand along my scalp.

I lean into her little face,
"It's still me."

She takes my hand and out we go
as she shimmies on her swing,
pumping higher, giddy as she
eats the day, "Look! Uncle Mark!
I'm swinging till I'm High
as the Sun! Look!"

I push her with all my heart,
"Me, too, sweetheart—"
she comes back to me—
"me, too."

LIFESONG WITH
TWO TRUMPETS

I am tired of those
who swill their head
in a bucket and claim
there is no God or Good
or Beauty to be had.

I come from a tribe
of survivors who love life
more than the hardships
they've been dealt. And
we have found each other
the way rivers find the sea.

We know pain, fear, and
struggle, like dark fish
nibbling at our bottom.
But have grown love, faith,
and will like barnacles,
razored out of sight.

We come from under
every sort of rock: drunk,
raped, abandoned, cancered.

And as we navigate our way,
everyone trembles at the
wheel, the cost of being real.

So I'm fed up with those
who suck at the dark side
of things, complaining
they are bored, complaining
life's a chore, complaining
there is nothing but their
chaos to applaud.

To be broken is no reason
to see all things as broken.

To fear death
is not a calling.

I have outlived a tumor
pressing on my brain, have
had my 8th rib removed, and
though I wept in the tub at the
gash in my side, at the fact that
I can be slit open so easily
like a bull pumped up for
market, I only want life
more, long to dance till
my heart sweats, till my
mind stops anticipating,
till I understand the dead
tree's part in the design.

I long like a root, deeper
in the earth, so I can reach
farther to the sky.

So don't tell me
there's nothing
in your bucket.

To brush my teeth has
significance after three
weeks of lying flat. And
there's glory in the water
from my mouth as it swirls
down the sink in rhythm
with the largest falls
I've never seen.

And when the missing
rib aches, I dream of
swimming naked in life's
waters with those who
pulled me back to this
season of mystery
so many refuse.

LETTER HOME

You ask if anything's changed.
I write this in an open boat
in the middle of a lake
which has been drawing me
to its secret for months.
I am becoming more like water
by the day. The slightest brace
of wind stirs me through.
I am more alive than ever.
What does that mean?
That in the beginning
I was awakened
as if a step behind,
always catching up,
as if waking in the middle
of some race that started
before I arrived, waking
to all these frantic strangers
hurrying me on,
as if landing in the middle
of some festival not knowing
what to celebrate, as if
someone genuine and beautiful
had offered to love me
just before I could hear
and now I must find her.
You ask if anything's changed.
I am drifting in the lake

and now it's a matter of slowing
so I can feel everything.

You say I don't sound the same.
It's 'cause I think more like a fish
and only surface to eat.
I used to complain so much,
annoyed that every chore
would need to be done again,
that the grass would grow back
as soon as I'd cut it. Now
I am in awe how it will grow
no matter what you do to it.
How I need that knowledge.
You say I don't try as much with you.
It's 'cause you still behave
as if life is everywhere
but where you are
and I need new knowledge.

It has not all been pleasant.
One of us died the other day.
The last time I saw him,
we held hands through a park fence—
he was thin—but we held on as if
the fence weren't there and as if
he were already on the other side.
Now we pray for him anyway, imagining
peace a lighter affair once gone
like pebbles sinking softly underwater.
I put my palm on the water's surface

lightly, not trying to hold any of it,
just feeling it push back.
You ask and I hesitate.
It seems everything has changed
when, in fact, it is only me.

I was closed so long, I thought
opening was breaking and in rare
broken moments I've seen now
how your secret is my secret
just swallowed at a different time
about a different face
with a different though equally
private name that brings it back,
too keenly, too deeply.

I write this in an open boat
where yards from me the heron
perched on turtle rock is spreading
its wings in the sun, holding
perfectly open and still,
the light filling, glazing its eye.
I am drifting here, heart spreading
like a heron's wing, more alive
than I thought possible.
You think me indifferent.
I want this for you
more than you can dream.
I am here. Drifting.
Come. Please. Swim.
If you can.

WHO WILL LIVE YOUR LIFE?

This is what the great choice comes down to—the great conflict between first-hand experience and tradition, between spontaneity and decorum, between compassion and obligation. Other life forms have no part in this. It's strictly a human affair. The sapling doesn't look to its elders for approval. It just grows toward the light. The bee feels its hunger and finds its honey. It doesn't embark out of any sense of duty.

When I speak of these things, distrustful minds, against all intention of getting involved, blurt out, *but we have to live in the real world*. After a long silence, I offer, *you must meet the outer world with your inner world or existence will crush you.*

And so it begins, continues, ensues: Who will live your life? The answer is obvious. Yet the difficulty is not in knowing the course, but in accepting the many ways we give our life away, accepting the many ways we abdicate the one outright gift we have.

Too often, we're told that to live in the real world we must give up our dreams in service of a survival that looms as pragmatic. In truth, it's the opposite. Living in the world in a real way requires the evolution of an interior life, and much of our health depends on how we, at our porous best, negotiate the infiltration of outer and the release of inner.

Kabir, the great mystic poet of India, suggests that the soul is merely a portion of ocean gathered in our pitcher of a life:

> Take a pitcher full of water and set it down on the water—
> now it has water inside and water outside.
> We mustn't give it a name,
> lest silly people start talking again
> about the body and the soul.

When we tend our soul, we tend to our portion of ocean. When we give complete attention to our portion of God's Being, we take up space and emanate the depths of our original energy. It's how we shine within. And at the edge, where the individual soul meets the world, where the pitcher meets the ocean, where inner light meets outer light, there is a kinetic border we can't resist, a rim called wonder that draws us back into the Whole.

But out of fear or pressure, or both, we often remove ourselves from life in order to handle situations. How often do we steel our feelings in order to act objectively? How often do lovers remove themselves from their field of intimacy in order to leave a relationship? How often do we inwardly sever our bond to a dear one who is ill, long before they're gone, to enable us to move on without the pain of losing them? How often do we minimize the life before us, so we can more easily do what we want?

We also stop living our own life when we succumb to the judgment and rejection of others. If you haven't encountered it yet, you'll surely be faced with the pressure of someone demanding more than you can safely give without damaging your soul. Whether that someone is a needy friend, an arrogant boss, an inexorable religion, or a perfectionist brand of self-justification, it all comes down to how each of us dares to say no when asked to be other than who we are.

And the violent speed of our age doesn't help. In a world so mobile and transient we can wake up married in Atlanta and go to sleep divorced in Fort Worth; the game has become who can snatch a mouthful of seed and be on their way first. In a world where sophistication means we show nothing, the mind becomes as cold as a camera shutter, opening and closing rapidly so as not to let too much in. In a world that makes a fortress of objectivity, we avoid the one frontier that returns us to first-hand experience: our ability to care. In a world that deems simplicity as dull, patience as slothful, and compassion as entangling, we give up inroads to our very core if we can no longer empathize.

Succumbing to speed is a form of isolation that makes us feel inadequate, because we're always falling short, always catching up. But stopping alone is not *entering* stillness, because stopping alone does not let who we are merge with where we are. Still, to stop and slow down is a beginning, because we start to find what matters when we stop rushing.

Rushing can be defined as any instance in which we move faster than we need to. As soon as we begin to rush, whether hurried by an overbearing parent to the dinner table or harried into a career choice by an artificial deadline of our own making, we become estranged from ourselves; that is, a hollow forms between our inner self and the self that's rushing through the world. Once divided from our sense of aliveness, we lose contact with that kinetic border called wonder. This estrangement from our aliveness is the beginning of alienation. And though there are many ways to feed our estrangement, rushing out of congruence—out of being where we are—is as sure a path as any to the netherworld of half-living.

If I learned anything from having cancer, it's that unless there's a physical need—such as needing air to breathe or needing to stop a wound from bleeding—there's no reason to rush, no matter the level of urgency being showered on us by others.

Each of us is driving our own train, and the trick is not to go so fast that everything blurs and yet to go steadily enough that we get somewhere; though there are times when not going at all is tantamount to arriving.

So who will live your life? Who will you dare entrust that to? Even when the Japanese poet Kikaku says,

A blind child
guided by his mother,
admires the cherry blossoms

the child does not relinquish the chance to admire the blossoms
directly. It seems the deepest love can guide or even lead, but then
removes itself as if it had never been there at all. Such a mother
barely touches her blind child's arm. Now the child can't tell if
the path to the garden was their mother's wind-like guidance or
the nudging of their own intuition. This is the gift of love.

Yet too often, we impose by giving what we so sorely need
or never received and, then, the child is made a puppet of
the giver's pain. When giving like this, we're driven by our
estrangement, hiding from the world while trying to expose
ourselves through others.

But who knows what a blind child sees when looking at
blossoms. Who knows what anyone sees from the privacy of
their own blindness. And make no mistake, each of us is blind
in a particular way as each of us has a unique sense of sight. In
effect, each of our fears blinds us to a particular depth. If we fear
heights, we are blind to the humility vast perspectives bring. If
we fear spiders, we are blind to the splendor and danger of webs.
If we fear small spaces, we are blind to the secrets of sudden
solitude. If we fear passion and involvement, we are blind to
the comfort of faith and the awareness of the Whole. If we fear
change, we are blind to the mystery of life. If we fear death, we are
blind to the majesty of the unknown. And since to fear something
is thoroughly human, to be blind is unavoidable. It's something
we keep struggling to overcome.

When we can slow down and move through our fear, we rejoin
the elemental force that resides in everything and are empowered
with a sense of original energy that reveals our gift. Such energy

enabled a poor, blind, orphaned teenager to find his gift and live his own life. I'm referring to Ray Charles who remarks:

> I was born with music inside me. That's the only explanation I know . . . Music was one of my parts. Like my blood. It was a force already with me when I arrived on the scene. It was a necessity for me—like food or water. Music is nothing separate from me . . . You'd have to remove the music surgically.

Regardless of the form this energy takes, we constantly struggle whether to honor the great flow of the Universe that empowers our very being or to fulfill our roles as prescribed by others. And while managing both can be done with a rare combination of skill and circumstance, more often, the effort to live what is expected blocks the flow of being we seek. After going deaf in 1792, the Spanish painter Francisco Goya understood this:

> To allow his genius to become apparent to himself it was necessary that he should dare to *give up aiming to please* [Andre Malraux].

The mystic Thomas Merton terms this the quest for integrity:

> Many poets are not poets for the same reason that many religious men are not saints: they never succeed in being themselves. They never get around to being the particular poet or the particular monk they are intended to be by God. They never become the person or the artist who is called for by all the circumstances of their individual lives.

So first there is the struggle to ignite what we are born with, which often requires withdrawing from the pulse of the crowd and all its demands. But we are more than a collection of skillful hermits. Our bond to others is as necessary to our well-being as our solitude is for inner knowing. As the psychologist John Bowlby says:

> Intimate attachments to other human beings are the hub around which a person's life revolves . . . From these intimate attachments a person draws [their] strength and enjoyment of life and, through what [we] contribute, [we] give strength and enjoyment to others.

It seems in living our life we are continually seeking the essence of relationship: of self to world, of self to other, of self to self, of self to the indescribable sum of these including the unnamable gradations of relationship in between which others have called God, Atman, Cosmos, Tao.

It's not enough to stay off unwanted influence. For while we journey alone, we are not the only ones on the journey. And while each journey is unique, we all journey over common ground. We all come from and feed off the same center. So it must follow: if we are to verify our own experience, we must honor each other's.

In the midst of his waterfall of genius, Mozart composed a very unique piece of music called *The Table Duet*. He wrote one set of notes on a single page, which could be read and played from either direction, from top to bottom or bottom to top. Read from the top down, one tune was revealed, and if read from the opposite direction, the bottom up, another tune was revealed. With the single sheet of music placed flat between two facing pianos, one player would read the page as right-side up, while the other would read a different tune from what they perceived as right-side up. Yet the same notes read from opposite vantage points would create a duet when played together.

Isn't this the paradox of true relationship? Isn't this the duet that earnest lovers ultimately play? Aren't we—in the dynamic of true intimacy—facing instruments butting up against each other? Isn't life an endless flow of moments that move between us like notes on the same page? Don't we experience the same things differently? Don't I always in my innocence and in my adherence to my own perception play back what happens to you upside down? Don't you in all sincerity play my joys and pains in a way that seems to reverse my intentions and reactions? Yet don't we play the same events, thoughts, and feelings together? Don't we, despite our struggles to be understood or understanding, don't we play *The Table Duet?* Don't we, through love, eventually understand each other? Don't we, through deep listening, turn noise into music? Don't we, by adding our voice, complete each other's story?

So who will live your life in relationship? If all we do is *aim to please,* we abdicate our capacity as a facing instrument and merely echo the stronger voice among us. Unable to withstand this struggle, many lovers either mirror their dominant partners or live alone. As in intimacy, so too in society: many citizens either abdicate their individuality by mirroring the wants of their culture or they withdraw into a self-imposed exile, living as a hidden warrior in a land of conformity.

Often, we experience our quests for personal truth and intimate attachment as opposing drives. For each human being, in pursuit of what it means to be alive, finds and climbs their mountain, again and again, like Moses, not sure what they'll find going up or coming back down. Yet in this journey into consciousness, into experience, into meaning and back to where we live, in this endless sojourn of exploration *and* return lies the test of our human greatness. For the masters, in love and art, whoever you think they are, are such because they do not cease to climb and seldom fail to bring the climb home.

And each trip takes longer by virtue of our growth. The longer the climb, the farther and more arduous the journey down and back. One reason the mystical poet William Blake is not fully understood is that he stopped coming back. By the Prophetic Books, he turned and kept climbing, never to return. In contrast, Wordsworth and Emerson spent more time at the foot of the mountain harking than climbing, which, in part, explains their attraction to Coleridge and Thoreau, who always stayed on the uninhabited side of the climb.

Truly, the task of human love is not to give up our exploration *or* our return. It seems the truth of relationship burns as the fire of our immersion in that pilgrimage back and forth from solitude to community, from spirit to flesh, from intuition to tradition. True relationship marks a kind of immersion into life we both crave and fear. After a lifetime of loving, it never ceases to surprise me how the act of relationship, like inquiry or honest thought, looks so treacherous before beginning, and so inevitable, like gravity, once on the other side.

But on this side, each of us is a blind climber looking for others while listening for the birds along the way. How often I've watched the geese discover one by one how hard it is to fly alone, how in the crisp October air they start to form their moving V, because each in aerial wake is boosted by the lift of the one before. And how the lead goose pumps the hardest till he tires and drops to the end where he can coast as another takes the lead. I watch this community of birds share the flight majestically and wonder why I don't even know my neighbor's name.

Yet if we dare to act in true relation—if we dare not to rush, not to live any faster than we are ignited from within, if we dare to slow into true presence the many times we do rush, if we dare to hear each other's needs, if we dare to accept the discomfort of not knowing what to do until it becomes the comfort of a perennial question—we might find that one life in its unmitigated fullness may be more than enough.

We might find, as the Taoist sage Chuang Tzu suggests, that hiding in itself is a great drain until we dare to live in our own skin:

> You think you do right to hide little things in big ones, and yet they get away from you. But if you were to hide the world in the world, so that nothing could get away, this would be the final reality of the constancy of things.

Throughout our lives, we struggle with the temporary ease of hiding and the pain of never surfacing: hiding our feelings of insignificance in our ambitions for a life of fame, hiding our confusions at the complexities of life in principles we hope will swallow them, hiding our pain of honest suffering in a resignation that stills the heart. And all the while our experience of what is real gets away from us.

But if we were to hide who we are in who we are, like hiding a body in its skin, if we were to let things be and not makeover their impact on us, all hiding would evaporate and the constancy of our self would be final, real, and unequivocal in its majesty of flaws.

When we can manage to live our own life, letting nothing real slip away, the larger ocean of life draws us with a magnetism all its own, the way a fish is drawn by light to a surface it can't imagine.

QUESTIONS TO WALK WITH

- In your journal, describe a time when you were chasing life and what that felt like. Then describe a time when life came to you and what that felt like. Describe the times you feel closest to life. How can you open to that feeling more often?

- In conversation with a friend or loved one, explore how love and suffering have loosened your grip on where you thought things were going. How have love and suffering affected your sense of will and control?

- In your journal, explore a way of thinking that isn't working any longer, one that is limiting your ability to experience life directly. What kind of new knowledge do you need in order to be more fully alive?

- A deep paradox of life is that no one can live your life for you, but no one can make it through life alone. In conversation with a friend or loved one, tell the story of a time when you experienced both sides of this paradox and how it changed you.

- In your journal, describe the one thing you stand on when the weather of life stirs up its storms. When things get rough, how do you find your footing? Ask this of a friend.

- In conversation with a friend or loved one, describe the difference between who you were ten years ago

113

and who you are now. What is the most important thing you've learned about life and about yourself during those ten years?

MIDWAY IN OUR JOURNEY

Just when we're softened by the years,
when we have enough experience to see
for ourselves, our maps are torn from us.
This can be frightening, but there's
divine timing in the dissolution of a
stubborn mind, the way an inlet waits
on the last rock to crumble so it can
find its destiny in the sea. Losing the
way set out by others is necessary so we
can discover for ourselves what it means
to be alive. Now we can burn the clothes
others have laid out for us, not in anger
but to light our way. Now we can let the
soul spill its honey on the unleavened life
we've been carrying. Now we can rise.

MAGNIFICENCE

I'm with burn survivors today. Fire has disfigured them. Changed them forever. Unlike the rest of us, their wounds can't be hidden. One has come for some wafer of hope. She is the same beautiful girl under all her taut scars. How she wants to go back to the day before the fire. Her pain is so great that she asks why God keeps her alive. What can you say to someone who feels the press of life that severely? She seems a ruined Atlas holding up a world on fire. I bow to her by not lying. We're not equipped to answer why or to venture that things will be better. Though they might. We can only bear witness to what it takes to still be here and to the mystical fact that nothing stays the same. These raw souls are tired and intense. Broken angels seared by falling too near the hot gears of existence. Fair? We drop below the human obsession with fairness and listen to each other's pain and talk about how to go on.

ANOTHER CHANCE

It's harder to hold onto things.
I've broken several bowls while
drying them, including the one of
a kind Nick gave my wife Susan.
Another chance to practice frailty.
I need to take more care in how I
lift, to let things settle in my palm
where I can feel them more than
carry them. And lately when our
dog eats too fast, she gets sick. So
now we squat beside her and make
her wait. She stops and chews and
we look at each other. These tender
moments opened by limits make
me stop in the market, watching
everyone handle fruit. I aspire
to stay tender. The softness of
light is everywhere.

NESTING

Last week, I was on a pier in Charleston.
There was a pelican, very close. I remem-
bered that pelicans make their nest by pluck-
ing feathers from their chest. The water kept
lapping and I felt illumined, for a moment.
Aware that you were home, medicating Mira.
Aware my father was on his side, unable to get
out of bed. Aware your brother, unable to choose
life, was again in jail. Aware that you are nesting
like a pelican in the middle of all this. Last night,
in the concert, as the guitars softened our worry,
I watched the light of the theatre quiet your face,
as I have for years, and thought, *I know we will lose*
things dear to us and it will seem impossible to go on.
And though the weight of grief we fear and master
looms like a dark god, I will be there when words
fail, to rub your feet and stir the soup, to
sweep up the slivers of pain that will come
from us. I know each thing we lose will cut
a string, but life is learning to play music
with the strings that are left. I took your
hand and closed my eyes. Aware that
the pelican so many miles away
was in flight.

I HAVE NOT FORGOTTEN

any of you. Not the long friendship we
somehow broke into pieces so sharp we
couldn't hold. Or the love we tried so
hard to mend though it splintered like
a fence we didn't post. I'm still not
sure what it was keeping in or out.

I have not forgotten the tender place
in which we met, where everyone gets
to put down the lies they've been told
are true.

I don't know where you are these days
but I burned the stories of our failure
along the way.

I hope you've been heard and held
since we were thrown so completely
into who we are.

The places we break don't seem to heal
as much as wear smooth, until what we
thought was principle crumbles like a
wall.

ON MY WAY

I'm on my way as the police
are pronouncing him dead.
And everything around him—
the IV, the bedpan, the doc-
umentaries he loved to watch,
the pills not yet taken—all of it
drops to the ground, like planets
without a sun. And my mother
leans on a chair in the kitchen,
her heart breaking wider than
she ever imagined. How to be
without him after sixty-seven
years. After all she and I have
been through, I will hold her
when I get there. I'll hold her
broken heart to the sun where
I can look into the canyon opened
in her, to see what she has guarded
all these years, to see where we all
come from and where we all will go.
Together, alone. I will hold her firm-
ly, gently, so she doesn't fall in.

Questions to Walk With

- In your journal, tell the story of a time that a life-map you had was torn or lost or just no longer accurate. How did you discover this? What did you replace the old map with?

- In conversation with a friend or loved one, discuss a limitation you have experienced and what it has taught you. Then describe a limitation that is challenging you now and what you think it might be asking of you.

- In your journal, describe a mask you have worn that you have put down. What made you put it down? What's the difference between living with a mask and living without one?

- In conversation with a friend or loved one, describe a time your heart asked you to put your history aside. In your life, when has history helped you know who you are and when has history kept you from yourself?

- In your journal, explore the difference you experience between pleasing others and being kind. Who taught you to please others? Who taught you to be kind?

- In conversation with a friend or loved one, describe how you make decisions. Tell the story of an important threshold you faced that stretched the way you usually make decisions and how that enabled you to get closer to life.

FACING THE RIVER

I have crossed this river before.
I almost drowned. One other time
it carried me to a new life. What now?
It's moving so fast I can't see myself.
Only the cries of others in the fast
water, pleading for me to come or
stay or go away. Funny how light itself
never moves but everything it touches
never stays the same. That's been my
love affair with truth. I wonder about
so many. Where is the sweet troubled
man who used to be my friend? Did
we stop caring? Or did the current
sweep us in different directions?
Nothing stands still in the water.
Or in life. Is that why we try so hard
to hold on? I keep breaking off what is
false so the irreducible thing at center
can show itself. I wish I knew the irre-
ducible thing's language. I know it's
trying to tell me something. Perhaps
the same thing for years.

BEING HUMAN

We're born with an aftertaste of Oneness
and a thirst for weeds and earth, as the angel
deep within us needs our hands, to make a
dance of all this hurt. It has us reach beyond
our limits, till we love like a planet though
we're constantly confused. We carry lightning
in a thimble of skin and bones and dreams.
We carry everything that matters in a plan
that doesn't last, while the stars pulse
to fill us, the way a candle fills a room.

As Moonlight

(For Ann)

When we began, we were eager to be loved.
Everything held wonder in a secret place
that was shouting like a waterfall.

I can't tell the whole story here
except to say that thirty years have passed
and we have been friends, lovers, have
saved each other's lives, been ex-lovers,
difficult friends, have felt discounted
and betrayed, have almost walked away,
have gasped onto the shore of forgiveness,
have found love in other eyes, and harshly
and sweetly, we have been worn
free of all names. We don't know
what to call each other.

Now, states away,
you are losing your sight
and I am creaky in the knees.

And I have cried in the midst of telling
what can't be told, sitting before strangers,
catching myself saying, "I found her injecting
a syringe in an orange. When I asked,
she said she was practicing how to
keep me from getting nauseous."

No way to sum up thirty years.
Or being pulled back into life. Or
being forced to bow to the changes
wrought by God's fugitive, time.

How do we talk to anyone about
what was held and dropped and lost
and still is always there. I swear I feel
eight and eighty at once. And you?
I pray you are well loved.

We are fallen limbs drifting apart
on the lake of nights, except as
moonlight paints our lives.

In the Back of the Eye

When I had cancer and Grandma died,
that silent explosion sent her away and
deeper into me at the same time. When
the sun came up behind that mountain
on the way to Santa Fe, I somehow knew
it was safe to creep back into the world.
And when afraid in every direction, the only
place my heart could chew was in the meadow
of now. It's as if we carry a very soft emblem of
the fire of life way inside, in the back of the eye,
and we're hardened to keep it from going out.
Then one day a bird we've never seen pokes
at the window and we think nothing of it
but everything within us knows it's time.
And the hardened places start to crack and
the heart stirs from its waking sleep. And all
the softness we've carried since birth is sud-
denly at the mercy of wind and rain. Now
when I see you rubbing your hand, I feel
all the things you've held. Now when I see
the snow cover the trees, I hear the story
of every tree. Now I'm forced to love every
walking statue until the thing trapped
inside can find a way out.

IN THE SEA OF OTHERS

It's next to impossible to do this
alone. We need the loving truth of
others to be well. Inevitably, some
come with us and are forever changed
while others watch as we're forced
out to sea. It's the power of love that
enables those who come along,
where a language of experience
is unearthed that can't be translated
to those who stay behind.

MOONGLOW

The moon on the frozen elm
was a lick of Eternity that said, *You
will go soon enough. Linger with
me.* And so I did. I stood there
till the cold crept into my boots
and the moon spilled up my face.
The thin blue shadows on the
snow were so bright it seemed
a day had stayed on to tame the
darkness from getting darker.
Then a sacred space opened
that I can't quite explain.

CHORES

I used to hate chores. Obsessed with imagining and creating, I had no patience for fixing or maintaining things. I've also been close to those equally obsessed with fixing, so much that they seldom experience anything new. Or so I thought. In many ways, I really had no use for the earthly life. Early on, I was a naïve mystic. Sensing grand moments of vision in which the vibrancy of the Infinite would blow through the veils of appearance, I only wanted to live on the other side.

But fifteen years of living, from my awakening as a poet to nearly dying of cancer, has made it clear that the duality between appearance and truth existed in *me*. The ephemeral quality of the Infinite was the result of *my* inability to see and feel its constancy. Clearly my eyes have been rearranged, for now I find the Infinite in *everything*. It's as if what matters has rooted itself behind my eyes, my mind, and my heart. Accepting this, I am budding as my sense of joy is taking root.

The wonder of being transformed is that we get to live more completely, more fully, *within one's self*. I've come to understand God as the force of Spirit that like the sun makes us grow into who we are, no matter what we have to go through. And just as the world perceived by a fetus does not change, though what it senses changes dramatically the more it grows, so too we, as we form new eyes, are born, first open them, and finally see. Once on the other side of such awakening, it's clear that the nature of the Universe remains the same. Clearly, I've become more integrated, forming new eyes. Clearly, my spirit has more thoroughly joined my body, birthing a different me. Clearly, my essence has melted more completely into the ordinary fact of my days.

My fantasies of God, once pure and directive, have melted, soaking like water into the even more glorious dirt. More glorious, because the Unity and Power of Life is *enlivening* this Earth. More glorious, because such Oneness defies the false separation of ideas from experience. More glorious, because such Wholeness defies the refuge of transcendence by which the fragile and the holy try to remove themselves from the abundance of what is, which is God *animating* the world.

So now I do the chores I used to hate, disliking them from the outside until my involvement takes me into the pure motion of my body lifting and holding the things of this world. My involvement takes me beneath the silhouette of mind that knows the task as a chore, in much the same way that saying the word *wind* long enough strips it of all familiarity. In this way, I do the chores slowly with full attention: tinkering, maintaining, fixing—doing all the things I vowed I wouldn't.

Just today, I found myself stepping through mounds of ensilage piled against the stanchions in a barn. The door to the manure-filled pen would no longer close. The barn had shifted over all these years, and the door was sticking on the concrete sill. I put hay on the manure around the door and knelt with a saw trying to cut the bottom of the door by half an inch. At first, I didn't want to do it, but there I was, caught in the motion of sawing horizontally. I could hear the cows chewing as I entered the rhythm, watching the saw's teeth rip further and further across the bottom of the door. And though wood cannot feel—at least not as we feel, or so we think—when pushing the saw faster than it could easily cut, I felt violent. When backing off and letting the saw glide in its own stroke, I felt so inside the sensation of sawing a door free that I suddenly felt the effort of others, in other times, sawing other doors free. Within minutes, I was so thoroughly sawing the bottom of this barn door that I could have been a carpenter planing Solomon's gate.

The day's earthiness returned, though it had never disappeared. As I stood, my knees were wet with manure and the door swung freely over a sliver of daylight through which the wind was now curling. I wondered if that sheet of air would chill the cows. I was amazed at how much light that cut sliver of wood let in.

It made me wonder: How do we shift over the years? How are our foundations eaten away? When beaten by the weather of living, how rough are we in the opening? And what then is the saw but the work of honest love: kneeling in our own manure or the manure of others, holding the broken gate firmly, and letting our honesty rip its stroke across the bottom of our door; till a sliver of light pours through, even when our door is closed; till we know ourselves by what shines through us.

I went into the house and collected all the garbage that would burn and lugged it to the rusty old barrel beyond the apple trees. It was muddy, and with each step I thought, there's something profound in this simplicity of carting used containers and old newspapers to the burning barrel. They lit easily, yellow flames opening like little shawls in which what they covered disappeared. I watched the cellophane that carried the perch all frozen from the sea. It dissolved to a clear shimmer that rose, as if the last motion of that fish rising for its hook was now being released. I watched the stories of brutality merge into smoke, saw the face of a child who'd been raped collapse into flame, saw her trust in anything join the shimmer of the perch. Saw the list of numbers we kept by the phone while Helen was dying curl, saw the doctor's -2473 unlink and char. Saw it all rise in a clear flame that softened the sky. And there, through the suffered clarity that only burning what is gone can bring, I found myself staring at a hawk who was watching from his limb, as if knowing it would come to this. His beak wavered through the clear heat, which now seemed a window. His wings were almost fluid. He seemed an ounce of God's elixir poured into the form of a keen bird, and I was glimpsing him just before he hardened into his life. I thought I saw the suffering, all burned and rising, coat the branch on which he stood. Through the flame, we were mirroring deeper parts of a larger self: he, the keen wing of memory hovering above the fire of all we have felt, and me, the hands of the future that must burn what can't carry itself. Then he moved. Higher and to the left. Once out of the flame, his eyes were merely clear, no longer all-knowing. He flew away, a hawk. I walked away, a man.

After lunch, I looked for something birdlike to fix and settled on the bluebird houses, whose openings must face south. They must stand alone at the edge of a field or the birds will never show. I tried to hammer new boards to the backs of the houses in order to fasten them to fence posts. The hammering was delicate: too hard and the houses fell apart, not hard enough and the backings wouldn't hold. I used old nails. They seemed more pliable. The houses once cleaned and backed were a bit rickety, but I trudged to the far end of the cow field and nailed them up as the cows thundered away. I stood and watched the oldest house pick up the wind, heard it enter the little bluebird hole and whip around inside.

I felt the wind whip through me and thought, how often we walk through it and never let it in. How much of our tiny lives is obsessed with shutting out and letting in. How we build and burn by turns. How we make things fit to keep the wind out. How we make things loose to let the light in. How much we like hinges so we can change our mind. And what made us ever think that building a small box with a little round hole would lure something blue to fly down from the sky? Why would something so free in the heavens seek such a confining home? And what strange paradox makes it hold true?

Is it that all existence is part of a balanced Unity which, like water filling a hole, flows from every part now full to every part

now empty? Is it that the bluebird in its divine innocence lives
a wisdom we struggle to maintain: that the air behind the hole
of the bluebird house is the same air in the heavens that the bird
flies so freely? Is it our inner task to regain the innocence of the
bluebird until we, too, can realize that the air behind the hole in
our heart is the same air that fills the Universe, until through our
heartfelt experience we live out our freedom to move between the
Universe within and the Universe without?

The houses must face south, the way the little hole in a
person's heart must face toward truth, the way each of us must
prop ourselves up in the open, our perforated heart open to the
wind. And there, we must wait beyond all logic for something to
fly out of the heavens and build its nest within us.

QUESTIONS TO WALK WITH

- In conversation with a friend or loved one, describe a chore you dislike and a chore you love. What's the difference? What makes one drain you and the other uplift you? What if the difference resides in you and not the chore? How might you turn chores into sacred tasks?

- In your journal, tell the story of someone you've journeyed with through a difficult time. What made you go on this journey? What was the gift of loving in this way? What was the cost?

- Sometimes the smallest adjustment can change everything. In conversation with a friend or loved one, tell the story of someone who changed a situation or relationship with a small gesture. Discuss how this happened. If that person is available, bring them into the conversation and ask them directly.

- In conversation with a friend or loved one, describe a time when a darkness you were in opened up. What happened around you or within you that shifted the density of the darkness? If lessening the darkness around us is a skill, how would you teach it?

- In your journal, describe a truth that slapped you awake. How did it surprise you? Where does this truth live in you now?

- Though a candle is a small light, it can fill an entire room. In your journal, describe someone in your life who is like a candle. Describe this person's light, and how they fill you. Describe your own light and how you can fill others. If you haven't told this person of their light and how it's touched you, tell them. Knowing the light, feeling the light, and praising the light is a deep form of medicine.

STILL HERE, STILL WONDERING

*Now that I've left the container
I have to stop being contained.*

MN

I f you are reading this, no doubt, you or someone you love is hurting or trying not to fall into the canyon of a loss. Not because life is oppressive but because it is mysterious and ever-changing. Yet somehow, we remain alive in spite of the breaks that surprise us, and in love beyond the accidents of time. Still, you might be struggling to restore your trust in life. Or someone you believe in might have lost their way. I hope that something in our journey to this point has been affirming.

After all I've been through, I can only say that it's the Wholeness of Life that renews us. The way the rush of a thousand miles of river lifts a tired fish at the mouth of the delta delivering it into the open sea. It's the rush of love that overflows our walls to break down the things we believe make us different. When I can give more than I think I'm capable of, then when you suffer, I suffer. When you can admit how little you know, then when you're made tender by beauty, I'm made tender. To live in wonder on the other side of suffering and disappointment is to know how magnificent and fragile it is to be here at all. Wonder is the key to restoring our trust.

The pieces in this section are personal accounts of my admission of frailty, my instruction from the great teacher that is limitation, and my vow to eat from the marrow of every moment without crisis or pain pushing me to remember I'm alive. The pieces in this section are testaments to wonder and the work that releases it. Most of these pieces were written in my fifties and early sixties. In "Unraveling the Self," I affirm how the path opened by expression leads us into meaning. In "Sifting Truth," I struggle to understand the tension between knowing our truth and enduring rejection, disapproval, and misunderstanding. In "Flint Work," I explore the constant need to remove the cataracts of mind that cover the pain and wonder of being alive. And in "The Bridge of Well-Being," I honor the inevitable call to be a bridge for each other, so we can endure what we suffer and inhabit the gifts we were born with, until we can enter the days that remain with awe and wonder.

The poems in this section have the perspective of having climbed to the rim of a canyon in whose river I almost drowned. Sitting on the edge, looking back into the dangerous, life-giving river while taking in the stars, there is only *amazement at being here at all and admiration for how suffering cracks us open, just in time to make us tender and ready to receive.*

Whatever path you're given, there is a bridge of well-being between us all that only the courage birthed by love can make visible. It is that bridge, always a step away, that leads us inside the miracle, which is everywhere.

Unraveling the Self

I would not be here, if not for a miracle, if not for a series of miracles. Every day when I wake, both death and life perch over my shoulders, and I get out of bed, simply glad to be here.

In needing to survive, I've been forced to pare my life down to what is essential, and in doing that, I've been transformed, and along the way, my sense of writing and living has transformed as well. It is about these transformations that I want to speak.

You see, a funny thing happened on the way to being a poet. At first, I was excited to bear witness to the mysteries of life. But, feeling chronically insecure, I kept returning to an unspoken need to be recognized for my efforts, and out of this, I grew an ambition to be great, the way a camel grows a hump. All of this twisted my journey to one of getting attention instead of giving attention, to seeking recognition instead of recognizing the life around me. I wanted to be verified for every poem I wrote, when the vitalities of life only reveal themselves to those who verify what is living. When most needy, I wanted to be great instead of being true.

All of this changed for two seemingly opposite experiences which stretched my sense of autobiography beyond just writing about my life to tending the ongoing relationship between writing (the life of expression) and living (the internal search for meaning) and how one continually affects the other.

The first experience was a vision for an epic poem that seized me when I was twenty-six and which took ten years to birth and create. This resulted in my second book, *Fire Without Witness,* a poem that explores the mythic and biblical voices that inhabit Michelangelo's Sistine Ceiling. This has been my deepest dive into the Unconscious. The whole enterprise was not about my life at all. I was called to explore a symphony of voices that I turned myself over to, putting my heart and mind and all my sensibilities into those characters. It was like pouring the water of my self into different shaped glasses. Yet, quite unexpectedly, doing so formed me inwardly and guided my life.

The voices and lives of these characters, when I could listen, became wise teachers. Turning myself over completely—by writing my way into the life outside myself—transformed me, enlarged me, humbled me, and healthfully broke my image of myself.

In fact, the unearthing of this material was even, in moments, prophetic. At one point, I imagined a tired Michelangelo tending a knot on a rib in his back, sore from hours of painting overhead; this, three years before I had a tumerous rib removed from *my* back.

This brings me to the other seemingly opposite experience that transformed me, my experience with cancer. Interestingly, as a poet, I was devoted to retrieving and surfacing my material, following the model of Michelangelo, who carved to release the statue already waiting inside the stone. But mysteriously, as life happened, I became the figure waiting in the stone, waiting to be carved and released by the hard sculpting of experience.

To my surprise, my cancer experience began to write me. Now I was desperate to stay alive, and so forgot about poems and manuscripts and publishers and overstatement. Now, I simply climbed a rope of expression, hand-by-hand, feeling-by-feeling, day-by-day, climbing my way into tomorrow. Now, my poetry became utter nonfiction. Here, the need to stay alive returned me to an expressive journey that drinks only of the Source. I was so busy surviving, I had no time to type and revise. It was only after surgeries and chemo and hair and no hair and months of repair that I found this rope of expression scribbled in journals. A few years later, it formed my third book, *Acre of Light*.

And so I learned rawly—through struggle—that the center we all share is the same, and whether we find our way there by going out of ourselves completely or by going into ourselves completely, either way, we must find that vibrant center of truth that waits beneath all names.

In this, we're left with an ongoing cycle in both writing and life, a cycle between self and other, through which we arrive, again and again, at mystery and meaning. In the life of writing as in the life of relationship, we must express our own authentic experience in order to clean the lens of self, so we might enter with full heart and mind the inner lives and questions of others, both real and imagined. Then, through the experience of others, we're called to better know ourselves, and on and on.

Not by chance, though often surprising, the giving over of ourselves to the expressive journey yields the next phase of our inner curriculum. For each life is a language no one knows. And with every heartbreak, discovery, and unexpected moment of joy, with every lift of music that touches us where we didn't think we could be touched, with every cut and confusion, another letter in our alphabet is decoded. Take a step, learn a word. Feel a feeling, decode a sign. Accept a truth, translate a piece of the mystery written in your heart.

It doesn't matter what mode of expression you're drawn to. It could be sewing, quilting, cooking, mountain climbing. It could be the art of listening or any act of service. Each creative act will lead us to our next teacher. Each form of expression will deepen our understanding of the language of our life.

Before we live what's next, we often think there's some answer we need to have in order to go on. But soon enough, we're humbled to discover, more than once, that the act of living itself unravels both the answer and the question. When we watch, we remain riddles to be solved. When we enter, we become songs to be sung.

With all this in mind, I'm moved to offer the notion that great work is an expression in which the author or artist or expresser is changed for having expressed it, is transformed for having encountered and released it. If and when this happens, it's inevitable that the work will be of use to others, in the same way that fire gives off heat.

So, you see, a funny thing happened on the way to surviving cancer. Without my permission, and with no decision on my part, my way of being as a writer was transformed. I woke on the other side, no longer driven to create something that never existed, but drawn now to bear witness to what has always been. I realized I'd been a make-aholic, a creative, even talented ball of energy whose worth depended on doing. But when I found myself awake in the struggle of a spirit expressing its trail, I began to find my worth in being. I had begun the shift from a life of achievement to a life of expression.

At first, without my drive, I feared I had lost my creativity. But over time, I came to understand that as a turbulent river finds its way to the sea, I had lost some of my noise and force, but had found more of my calm and depth.

From this unexpected depth, all my endeavors appeared to be connected. Both the artist in me and the spirit in me were finding expression through each other. By writing about others, I could learn about myself. Then, by writing about myself, I could learn about others or the other way around. Now, it seems that characters and voices and aspects of the self are just lenses for unfolding the mysteries of life. For characters are just extensions of self, known and unknown, and each face of self is just another character. Fiction, poetry, nonfiction: I'm coming to see that all the genres are just different brushes used on the same canvas.

Ultimately, my experience as a poet and a cancer survivor forced me to enlarge the notion of autobiography to encompass an ongoing dialogue with the dynamic Oneness of Life from which we keep learning what our particular contribution is to be in our time on Earth.

Whether we're exploring the lives of so-called fictional characters, or whether we're giving expression to the fabric of our suffering in so-called nonfiction, or whether we're plucking the harp strings of the inner world in the music of our poems—in each effort, we're adding to the emerging myth of our people, drinking from the same common well at center that has fed every generation.

In truth, writing about our lives, if done with sincerity and a devotion to reality, is the wellspring from which the particular gifts of humanity flourish. When we write about ourselves deeply enough, we write the world, and when we enter the world fully enough, we write ourselves. In this way, we live out the paradox of being both unique and the same.

By trying to create, we are created. By trying to express, we are expressed. By trying to discover meaning, we become meaningful. So the measure of great art can be understood, not so much by the singular beauty achieved in birthing a piece of art, but more by the power of transformation it births in us for the journey of creating it. It is not the thing created, but the creative act—whatever form it might take—that restores us to our place in the Mystery.

CRACKED OR HEALING

On the other side, everything,
from the quick song of birds
to the peace trapped within
a brook's fresh gurgle,
everything is rare
and uncertain.

Now I want to stand naked
before every wind, though
I fear I will break.

And all the warrior selves
stand guard, well-trained
for the next crisis: the fingers
search the glands during winter colds,
the eyes trace scars for irregularities,
the heart tightens like a lip
when entering a hospital,
where the unfelt part of my
journey cries like a babe
wanting its strange milk
when seeing needles
hang from brittle arms.

But underneath, the oyster
of my soul lives like a Queen
dethroned and exiled for her softness,
though everything that matters
seeps into her cell.

I wait for her to send the guards
away, but with a sort of pity
she lets them occupy their time.
What else would they do?

I have given up the world
through her. It peels
like bark.

Through her
I imitate the moon,
lighting the night
with reflections
of my craters.

Survival is the standing watch.
But living now is blessing every crack
as an opening, treasuring the song
that whistles through as God, praying
the break to let Him in
won't end it all.

FOR NUR

I've been terribly busy since
you died, fingering my list of
things to do like a rosary, veiled
in a shroud of activity, afraid to
let it in, afraid your death means
I am dying too, and when that's
passed, sad to think I might
go on undaunted
without you.

After months of furious doing,
of painting and planting, after
mornings of pondering ancient
philosophy, I had my own checkup
and in brief moments feared I was
you, but as the CAT scan whirred,
I knew I was well and strangely
let you go, your presence
drifting on its own in the
sea that holds us both.

Now your father calls.
He's packing up your things
and says you wanted us to choose
something you held close,
but each of us will sigh,
it was me, as we rummage
through your things

the way orphans comb
the attic of their past.

You were always well,
deeply well, no matter
the condition of your skin.

This morning the busyness is
gone and I watch the wind move
through the oak, its leaves
astir.

Everything seems closer,
renewed, and the part of you
where I held on has fused
like broken bones growing
white across their break.

LOVE-SUFFERINGS

When I began writing poetry, I almost studied with a tough fiber of a man, Paul Blackburn, but he died of cancer. It shook us all. Later, I read how he regarded his plight, "I want no pity for a pain I would share with no man." I was disturbed. I didn't understand. And now, after having tread my own yard of hell, I still don't understand. Pity is to love what sarcasm is to honest speech, but sharing pain is the only way to stay alive. I am sorry he felt so all alone.

Perhaps when we almost die, we empty our pockets too fast and perhaps too late, but there is no shame in empty pockets or empty moods. And while needing love to feel good about being alive is a modern indulgence, needing love to stay alive is the archetype behind God almost touching Adam's finger. Perhaps, in the original sense of séance, death can be put off if we simply join our love in earnest expectation that we be touched from the beyond.

I have never wasted my gift. Now, I've had to fight for it. I still am. But not alone. Rather with a net of love which helps absorb and distribute the struggle. It's taught me that if we share pain, which is a lot to ask, there is no room for pity. For sharing the struggle requires an investment, a real life-changing investment by those who care, an involvement that will instigate their own tandem suffering. Pity is a bleacher activity. It is the substitute for front-line caring.

I am well today, because those who love me got involved, deeply involved, daily involved. And by being so healed, I am forever wed to their pain. I am forever open to their struggles. By being so loved, I can never shut my life completely again. If they fall, I will live lower. If they rise, I will take on their dizziness. We will live like pools of water, each clearly individual but all sharing and exchanging the same slippage and rush of tides. Now I understand. This is the basis of human family, the sharing of pain, the investment of love by which we make a difference and are changed, again and again.

I have said throughout this ordeal, repeatedly, "Come with me, if you can, as far as you can." It was a plea for help and company. And from those who've come along, I've learned that touch is the clearest way to know another's experience. To walk through the surf makes us part of the ocean. To watch it swell and recede makes us just a shiftless though sympathetic dune. I am well because people didn't watch my suffering, but entered it; through which they felt love-sufferings of their own; which, at times, hurt them too much; which, in turn, forced me to nurture them; until, in bare, essential ways on certain days, we weren't sure who was ill and who was well. A solution that saved us all.

SOFT AS SATISFACTION

We often pray God will let us have truth.
It is more important to pray God will help us live with it.
ROBERT PENN WARREN

I was so solid when our lives were crumbling.
Why am I powder when you and the days
are sturdy as gold?

I am fading into ordinary ways: mere scratch
of belly, long itch of eyes.

I knew all through it, if all else failed,
my compassion for the Whole like an atom of
nectar would fight off death and bring us
back, for a while.

But now, the days seem unmagnified
without emergency. Why can't I be brave
when mere silence is at stake?

I have been fighting the passage
into normal life the way a salmon,
hooked and set free, tires
and starts to slip downstream.

Names and praise no longer feed.
But more, what scares
is the lack of hunger.

LETTING GO

After feeling driven my whole life
something very near the center has
unwound and I can no longer hurry
through airports or return all my calls.

And sometimes people I barely know
swim up like old worn fish to show me
the map of their gills, and the one long
gash of something they once swallowed,
and how it has cut each breath since.
And I am honored to warm them
like a blanket. But when alone, I
find it hard not to watch
what I swallow.

When alone, these things
I've wanted to know since birth
feel so unanswerable, I must
have been torn from them.

I'm sure a hawk doesn't know it's a
hawk. I'm sure a spirit doesn't know
it's being spiritual. Or a screen door
slapping, like a tired life, in the night,
if it's opening or closing.

Though we give up the murky fears,
we still can't know our worth, any-
more than a faceless treasure
can fathom why
it was boxed
or buried
or saved.

INSIDE THE MIRACLE

Great knowledge sees all in one.
Small knowledge breaks down into the many.
CHUANG TZU

Like the deepest wind, the unnameable miracle will move us all and remain unseen. I know this siege is over. We are being rocked into the days. And I know already that just as everyone wanted to blame this illness on their partial understanding of disease: it's in your bones, in your food, in the synthetics of your home, the vinyl of your Pontiac, in the emptiness of your life; it's in your protein, in your spinal fluid, in your lack of vitamins; it's in your sexuality, in your stress, in your family, your century; it's in your water, in your air.

Just so, already, I can foresee that everyone will claim the tumor's disappearance for their partial understanding of wellness: it was Jesus; it was Moses; it was our collective prayers; it was the strength of your mind; it was your visualization, your writing, your goodness returning to you; it was the technology of the day, the medicine of the day, the expertise of your doctors, your change in diet, your change in outlook, your ability to endure, your ability to submit, your ability to take charge, your capacity to accept; it was our love for you; it was your love of life.

Just so. It has been our lot since the conception of consciousness to praise what we are and blame what we are not. Yet I have been blessed to have a Catholic priest lay his brooding hands on my Jewish head. I have had a woman I've never met lead a Sufi meditation weekly on my behalf. I have had an artist paint his version of Michelangelo to give me strength. And a poet made a bookmark of sweet grass meant to heal. And I have had deep friends pull crystals from the earth and wash them for me to carry as protection. And yet another has given us a petal from the Philippines which appeared in a miracle in 1948. And old friends in New Hampshire have designed a cancer-free diet, which they are assuming with us. And my brother is insisting that I exercise and consume vast quantities of vitamin C. And a kind woman who has loved us from afar enrolled us both in the daily prayers of yet another religious order in Massachusetts. And a sweet friend who does not believe in God sits with me in silence when I have nothing left to say. And still another dear soul is praying to her dead mother and to Thomas Merton that we be healed. And I even talk to Grandma sometimes or visualize my cells repairing as I sit in her golden chairs.

Just so. I am blessed that all these efforts carry me. For each is indispensable. Just so. I need Catholic, Jew, Mystic, Sweet Grass, Sufi, Herbs, Crystal, Dead Mother, Dead Grandmother, Dead Monk, and Golden Chairs to heal.

I only know that everything has helped, and I am not great enough or wise enough to break down into percentages how much vitamin, how much medicine, how much prayer, how much God, how much Jesus, and how much mental fight. I only know that those who suffer partial belief are only partially healed.

QUESTIONS TO WALK WITH

- In your journal, tell the story of a time you lost trust in life and how you restored that basic covenant. This is important to understand as the losing and regaining of our trust in life will continue to happen, as part of the cycle of life.

- In conversation with a friend or loved one, describe a time you learned more about yourself by delving more deeply into others. Then describe a time you learned more about others by delving more deeply into yourself.

- In your journal, tell the story of a crack that turned into an opening. What cracked? What opened? What did you lose? What did you gain?

- In conversation with a friend or loved one, speak about a time of emergency and how that concentrated your awareness and describe your shift of awareness once the emergency passed. How do you stay awake now without emergency prodding you?

- In conversation with a friend or loved one, describe the most sincere person you know and what you admire about them. Discuss what keeps you from being more sincere.

- In your journal, explore what you need to give up or put down in order to take the next step in your journey of healing.

SIFTING TRUTH

I remember being nine or ten at a lake in the Adirondacks where a distant friend of my father's had come to visit. I'd never seen him before, and I have since learned he was a fugitive of sorts. I remember watching him on the early morning dock staring into the lapping water, staring more deeply than anyone I'd ever seen. He didn't know I was watching, but when my foot snapped a twig, he came back immediately and I could tell he was used to coming up when others were around. I wanted to know what he saw and, with hesitation, I asked. He looked at me and chuckled. I stood quietly still. I knew he had seen something special in the water. He got up, patted me on the head, and muttered, "You'll have to see for yourself."

Ever since I've been intrigued with two questions: how we know what we know, and how we share what we know. By the age of thirteen or fourteen, I experienced an adult giving himself away. I was at my first school dance, and a young music teacher was trying so hard to belong to a group of older teachers that he was saying almost anything, changing his demeanor and his views in an effort to be accepted. I only caught glimpses of conversations about subjects I didn't understand, but somehow it seemed very clear what was going on.

It seems, at times, we're so impressionable in our personality that our bane is how we turn chameleon, offering up our vision for an ounce of love. At other times, we're so impressionable in our being that our blessing is how we transcend the yoke of selfness, dispersing for the moment into a confluence of grace. And so by the age of fifteen I had learned that some great ongoing struggle awaited. Only years later could I give it words. It seems to me now a constant polarity of yearning: the fending off of influence so that unencumbered reality can reach us with its truth *and* the abating of loneliness at having a mouth full of light and no one to kiss.

In Japanese, the word *sumu* means both "to live" and "to be clear." And part of the mystery of being human stems from the inexplicable fact that clarity arises most often in solitude. Much to our short-lived ecstasy and long-term frustration, some of our deepest, most alive moments occur when alone, when pruning away the thoughts of others like weeds that block our path to light.

But being alone with either clarity or confusion compels us to voice our sense of abundance or emptiness, as if keeping either to ourselves for too long will turn the stuff poisonous. This is why confession works. Though the church has diluted its meaning, the urge to confess—to share secrets and truths, to voice in the presence of another what we've found or what we haven't—is empowering. Sadly, this is all that's left to the homeless who often publicly confess their deepest emptiness to their collective other walking by.

It's interesting that in Japanese the word *naru* means both "to become" and "to sound." So, if to live is to be clear, to become is to sound or express what is lived. And while a bird sings for no audience, a lion roars for its mate, and a widowed whale emits deep melancholies as it searches the ocean for its other half. So, while not always necessary, expressing what is lived implies expressing it to another. It implies being heard and received. For while experiencing something freshly is exhilarating, being heard is validating. Just as our heads are free to the sky while our feet are kept to the ground, our feelings are free as they are felt, but their reception is inevitably grounded in the hearts of others. Ironically, both are necessary to sustain meaningful living: the act of feeling and the reception of feeling, both of which involve expression.

Yet why—though it is always so—why is the cost of being heard attachment? Why do we feel bound to the one who has heard? Perhaps it's God's way of pollinating the best of our secrets. Perhaps our need to be heard causes us to bond with another, long enough for a tireless energy to be released, as when molecules bond to deepen the color of an orchid. Perhaps the exchange of clarity we know as being inside another's skin is the result of a metaphysical union equivalent to intercourse through which we conceive and propagate spirit.

Whatever the case, a deeply intrinsic nature drives us into the lives of others where being heard and received verify our existence, while being attached begins to erode our most private self in both healthy and unhealthy ways. When healthy, our attachments fuse like the arms of Egyptian lovers entwined so long that when unearthed they are thought to be one. But when our attachments preclude what is central, we are diminished as when a spouse never lets their loved one venture far enough to have a separate experience to share.

The native task—of being and becoming, of living clearly and sounding fully—is sorely exacerbated by our social and moral imperatives to fit in. Ironically, we make heroes of true individuals in retrospect, while censuring true individuality when we meet it on the street. For human history has always swayed in its want to stand apart and its want to belong, in its want to live clearly in solitude and its want to sound fully in the company of others.

We're stirred by mismatching urges: one nudging us to follow our clarity till we experience Unity, the other monitoring the degree to which our sounding will be tolerated. It's enough to make a pilgrim schizophrenic: feel it all, but keep it to yourself. It breeds a painful tension that no one seems able to escape. On the one hand, we're born with a trust in the interior life that it will serve as a threshold to the Universal Ground of Being. On the other hand, we're taught to be skeptical of a brutal world overrun by those afraid of the power of truth. At our worst, our communities are so frightened by the energy of truth that we ostracize, exile, or harm the pilgrim who shares it, as with Gandhi and Martin Luther King Jr. And it's important to remember that, on any given day, we are both: the seeker and the one who pushes the seeker away.

For most of us, this leads to a tense state of living in which the modern pilgrim in search of Unity is open internally and guarded externally, until we become, by turns, an inlet to nature and a fortress to others. Perhaps this is what led Goethe to remark: "Tell a wise person or else keep silent."

Today, the plight of the spiritual seeker often involves a tandem effort: socially closeting one's self like a spy, afraid of being caught and ostracized by our virtuous brothers and sisters, while privately opening our most private self to the Eternities, hoping to catch a mist of light that might anoint our soul. In this way, we all develop secret identities and become hidden heroes in our own comics. Why else are the people we work with so different when we chance upon them in the world?

But the real danger of skepticism is the erosion of trust. Not only in what we hear, but slowly, eroding back into the ground of our own perception until we can't trust what we see, until we ourselves stop living clearly, until we become unreliable in our own interpretation of what we experience.

Deep distrust is corrosive to our mind. Bad experience— rejection, disapproval, and misunderstanding—initiates distrust, and often, it is warranted and understandable. But while lack of trust prevents us from being heard and received, it also prevents us from sounding fully, and this keeps us in isolation with the few gifts we've retrieved. Because no matter how justified in the beginning, sustained lack of trust starts to erode the

clarity of our first-hand experience, coloring our perception
with doubt. This is akin to a liar not knowing who to believe.
For very subtly, when steeped in distrust, regardless if we're
right or wrong, we are, with nary a blink of the heart, not just
skeptical of others, but suddenly in interior crisis as we're now
more skeptical of ourselves. And since at the core we're all one,
when we distrust another without cause, we doubt that part of
ourselves, and such doubt spreads like rot in wood till the center
turns punky.

Yet all the while the Unity of Things is relentless in its lure,
demanding more trust than ever, demanding that we do exactly what
we fear we can't, demanding that we loosen our grip, that we let go
of what we're so afraid to lose. Thomas Merton puts it this way:

> A [person] cannot enter into the deepest center
> of [themselves] and pass through that center into
> God, unless [they are] able to pass entirely out of
> [themselves] and empty [their self] and give [their
> self] to other people in the purity of a selfless love.

But when out of balance and skewed by the infection of
skepticism, this selfless love waits in the open like a home on
the other side of a canyon that seems impossible to cross. And
Everywhere—*Other People!* Intimate and Strange! Calling and
Ignoring! How? How to sound from within, in the face of others
who want nothing of what's been found? How? How to live with
others? How to live without them? These questions never go away.
And now, as well as preventing the influence of others, there's
this skepticism turned inward which dirties our lens. Eventually,
it keeps us from both living clearly and sounding fully, leaving
us, as Rilke complains, in a shadowed state, half-connected to
everything, fully bonded to nothing:

I am too alone in the world, and not alone enough
to make every minute holy.

And grasp as we will, nothing comes through cleanly, nothing
pulls apart neatly, nothing that is digested is simply itself, as
if the Source in its coagulated variety insists on giving us
morsels beyond what we have asked. As the naturalist John
Muir discovered:

When we try to pick out anything by itself, we find it
hitched to everything else in the Universe.

Frustrating as it seems, this ingestion of diversity is our path back
to trust, which will bring us back to Wholeness, if we can risk the
wall of our own skepticism all mortared with our wounds. It is how
searching for one thing, you find another, how driving to escape
your own thoughts, you come upon a lone heron fifty yards away,
and you stare at each other for the longest time until the heron
leaves with the only piece of yourself you still want, and now you
have to face what's left, the part of your mind you've been avoiding.

But if we manage to avoid ourselves further, the pain hardens
and the wall solidifies until our distrust of others contaminates
our perception even further. Then, if unresolved, we twist what
we see to soothe our pain until, as the Jewish philosopher Martin
Büber suggests, "the manufactured has been mixed with the
received." Until what we make up dilutes the truth of what is.

It reminds me of my first fall in love. She left me bruskly.
And for such a long time I saw rejection behind every invitation
until my ability to perceive kindness was undone, until I began
to rationalize the world to muffle my pain, until one day I heard
myself conveying my own story falsely, to an innocent stranger,
telling how it was I who left her.

Oh why is none of this simple? Why the pull in all directions? Or is it that we are better equipped for experience than understanding, more aptly disposed to the logic of the senses than the physics of the mind? To a Russian, his alphabet is basic; to an American, the Russian word is unrecognizable. To a pilgrim of the heart, the ways of paradox are fundamental; to a pragmatist, foreign and useless. And part of the pilgrim's protection is the camouflage of uselessness.

This problem is not peculiar to our age. As far back as 300 BC, the Taoist sage Chuang Tzu tells the story of the oldest living tree and how it was scorned by every carpenter as being too gnarled and knotty to be of any use, not even good for firewood. Yet whenever they would leave, the tree, over two hundred feet tall, would boom back with the full power of its voice:

> Every other brother that was of use is gone. It is by
> my *not* being of use that I survived beyond your axe.

Perhaps the reason our youth are resistant to overly directive education is that they fear being used up as firewood by a society that doesn't value them. Perhaps we as a society have bred a child who feels that the only way to survive is to be of no use. Perhaps the gnarled and knotty rule has become: to be an individual means to be an outlaw, to grow beyond all recognizable use.

In effect, there are hidden tribes of youth today who hone their selfhood as a tool of survival, as a shield to survive the socialization of school. When schools function as fueling stations for values, pumping empty tanks full of prescribed virtue, young people are rarely allowed to explore their deep tendency to Unity. In truth, many teachers and administrators operate like pilgrims turned spies, rarely showing who they really are. In actuality, the role models in schools, very often, are simply those who hide more effectively, who survive more discreetly.

Carl Jung in the 1950s warned that the West is slowly living a deadly paradox; that while American society admires the rugged individual and can't exist without the individual, the monolith of our society has only one appetite, to eliminate the individual. We are creating a misanthropic beast that despises itself.

Yet if these things are true, our task is as grave for ourselves as for our society: to restore our trust and usefulness without being crushed. But how? During the Tang Dynasty, Lu Yen, more commonly known as Ancestor Lu, believed that:

> The Tao is entered by way of sincerity . . .
> Before practicing the art of immortality,
> first practice the art of humanity.

But what does it mean to be sincere, if not first-hand in all contact with the world, if not shield-free, mask-free, veil-free. Indeed, to be sincere is to strive for nothing to exist between inner and outer. Needless to say, this requires courage and compassion. And to enlist these qualities we are brought back to the resurrection of trust. As I write these lines, I can see my Grandmother's face the last time I saw her. She was ninety-four and could barely breathe, and as I left, as she thought me gone, I paused in the hall and caught one last glimpse when she thought no one was looking. And in that moment I could tell by her century-old face, she was a soft membrane thinning between inner and outer seas. More than ever, her face was full of trust. She opened her neck to God and closed her eyes.

As Lu affirms, it's through this kind of sincerity and trust that people can make the extent of their minds reach everywhere and encompass everything, so that all living creatures are embraced within the mind of the individual.

Like a ribbon of wind that gusts and circles the smallest leaf, all rests on this immeasurable thinness called sincerity. And in order to grow useful, which is not always synonymous with being productive, we somehow must discover our true place, not as instructed by others, but as uncovered by the litmus of our own uncorrupted sincerity. As the psychologist Rollo May asserts,

> Anxiety comes from not being able to know the world you're in, not being able to orient yourself in your own existence.

Dare I say it: the risk to be sincere will find us our place, and once in place, which can happen anywhere, our tendency to Unity will empower us with a holistic use. The kind that humbles the part with its being inconsequential and yet indispensable to the Whole, the kind of understanding of purpose that has an old soldier drop his gun and stare into the sun as he realizes his place in the scheme of things.

Still, the quandary of relating to others. Legend has it that in the 1300s, after spending the first half of her life in a convent, Catherine of Siena was called by God to enter the world. She questioned, "Why? How?" Jesus came to her in a vision and said, "There are two commandments. Love God, and love your neighbor as yourself. You have only done the first. You cannot walk with one foot. You cannot fly with one wing." And so she entered the world, aspiring to be integrated: loving the God in others and the God in herself until the commandments became interchangeable, until loving others was loving herself was loving God.

All very nice, but still no clue as to how. This brings us back to Martin Büber who recalls walking through a meadow at dusk, and as the light vanished, he moved with his walking stick toward the trunk of an oak. Slowly, he reached out with the stick till it was perched between his palm and the thick bark. He could feel the skin of the tree in his hand, and in that skin-bark moment, *living dialogue* occurred to him. For it seemed clear that he was, through the feel of that stick, in two places at once—in himself and in the tree. The stick made it so, conducted it so. Through the stick he could feel that oak. Then he realized, the stick was no different than the genuine conduit of true speech, a bridge placed directly between two living things by way of a lasting impression of light.

How to live like this in our palms? How to be so fully where we are? Can genuine direct exchange let us feel the bark of who we're talking to? Can sincere perception let us touch with our eyes? I believe so, for when, by courage or accident, I've found myself nakedly in dialogue with another, we uncannily enter into the Way of Things. It seems simple enough, if not always simple to find. Through the same sincerity with which we risk entering the Whole, we must risk the very thing we often fear, that is, the unpredictable impact of another.

Büber dares to propose that dialogue between us can be as real and unrehearsed as our private moments of perception. But how to even try? Lu says simply, be sincere. But are they mad? Don't they know what waits in the indifference of others? Don't they know about the pain of not being heard? Don't they—*This is not about they, but about us, about you and me. And we, as our former selves before us, face these dilemmas, over and again: To go off like a Navajo warrior on some vision quest where no one, not even the history of our own mind, can interfere, and to return with trepidation and a burning at the base of our heart to share all the unspeakable things. And we, as all others before us, face the* cost of doing neither. We can deny the quest for vision and so, never live clearly. And we can shy from saying the unspeakable and never sound fully. Or we can live impaired, inhibiting half of what we're given, like a seer with one eye or a lover with one arm.

At best, we can inquire directly of each other and wash our questions like tired feet in the pool between us, careful, as Chuang Tzu warns, that:

> if you probe, do so in a part
> where (the) skin is not sore.

There is no not wanting the clarity. There is no escaping the confusion. There is no not wanting to be heard. There is no escaping the loneliness. At best, we can search alone together, bringing fuel to our common fire and food to our common pot. At best, we might wander a mountain in spring intoxicated with its flowering cherries, bursting in our solitude as the twelfth-century pilgrim Saigyo did when he wrote:

> if only there were
> someone else
> willing to bear this loneliness—
> side by side we'd build our huts.

SUSAN MEANS LILY

While the rest of us work to re-
move what stands in the way, you
are quietly burned by the intensities
few of us feel. When we drive by a
dead fawn, I see the carcass, but you
see the fawn as its life left its body.
You feel the deer breaking in air.

After a storm, I see the old maple
split, fascinated to see the inside of
anything. But you somehow feel the
tree snapping. Others whisper,
"She's too sensitive."

After all these years, I know you
have no choice. You're one of those
born with no skin but your heart.
You can't turn it off. It's why I fell
in love with you. Why I learn from
you and care for you by turns.

How many times I've hovered,
wanting to see what you see and
feel some of what you feel. How
many times I've wanted to keep
you from the pain of having no-
thing in between. I can't. So I hold

you in aftermath and trail you like
a blind singer kissed awake by a
breeze hiding in a woman's body.

When the world breaks, you turn
into a butterfly. I worry that your
wings will be torn by the rain.

SITTING NEAR A SMOKE BUSH

I t was feathery and in bloom. Bees were circling. Children were playing. Paper plates were blowing across the lawn. He said his father's passing was hard and ugly. Sometimes, he wondered if loving others was worth it. It was clear by how his face softened that this was offered by someone who can't stop loving. We shared some more history. It's true, I thought, the cost is great, but without loss and joy prying our inner eye open, we remain blind.

We talked on. I meant to say how resilient we are, that there's no end to what we can endure or create out of love for each other. We talked about our immigrant families and what they'd overcome to simply cross the sea. We talked about our brothers who showed up during our cancers in ways they never had.

It seems we're always given a chance to enter life and stop watching, a chance to cross an imaginary line that we think separates us. It might be a step that rings through the world—like Nelson Mandela singing after being beaten or Rosa Parks staying in her seat or Gandhi beginning his march to the sea. But often, what moves us to take that step is more quiet, though no less brave—like those Swedish citizens putting the Star of David on their coats so the Nazis couldn't sort out the Jews. Or it might be what causes us to speak to those no one else will talk to, because they're different or homeless or dying.

We both looked off, knowing exactly where that line waits for each of us. We drifted in silence for a while. And on that lawn, under the shade of a fairly young tree, while others were eating and laughing and the cat was trying to shimmy under the blanket, I admitted that when I fear I won't survive one more breaking—just then I break. When I'm convinced I can't endure one more version of pain—I'm pained into something deeper. Always opened into something more fundamental. This is the miracle of being broken or loved open. We're constantly led into a world that keeps opening.

Slowly and sweetly we fell back into the lives we arrived in. I'll probably never see him again. But briefly, we paused in the river of our days—two fish slapping in the water—wondering where the current is taking us.

SNIFFING FOR YOU

Oh Steve, when Jill called
Susan answered. It was late.
I could sense something had
happened. She leaned over, in
shock, and said, you died. I fell
from the couch. We all called
each other, staring into the phone,
thinking of Pat and how she found
you. I woke early today, hardly slept.
I just walked Mira under the moon,
wondering if you're already part
of its light. I went to one knee to
smell the earth and rub Mira's
chest and thought of your dogs
sniffing for you.

FORGED

When the pain closed its fist,
I became a silent scream. When
the needle entered, I parted like
water. When the moonlight said
it was over, I relaxed into sea
grass, bending to its whisper.
Then the voice inside changed
languages and I became unknown,
faceless as a stone, relieved to be
smoothed. When you picked me
up, I became a dove, everything
aflutter. To be human is to resist
and become everything we meet.

IT

First It was a woman with auburn hair
whose head would moan when I'd kiss her neck.
Then It was a game where despite the others
I would rise in the air and toss the ball
as if it were all that mattered of me
and I'd only feel complete when it
slipped the net, touching nothing,
just falling blissfully from the sky.
Then It was a solitude that overwhelmed
me, on a mountain, or lingering by a brook
longer than the others. Or talking for hours
till the words were strewn like clothes and
there was nothing to repeat. And then It was
Grandma wearing down to a precious set of bones
and I made pilgrimage to hear her secrets once
she could no longer speak. And when you went
into surgery, I fogged the sliding doors,
watching your stretcher grow smaller,
believing It was thinning there
between us. But now, I am rightfully
tired of the chase and It has changed,
as have I, from something outside of us
we reach for, to something that was deep
within all along. I've stopped asking
for things to emulate, have stopped pushing.
Some say I am getting old. Even so, I can't
find the words in stream or sky to make clear
what I've found. Just stay near long enough

and my eyes will tell and we will both
let down, unsure what to do next. This
is a sign. For It is *here, in us* as we
bend. Oh how this life unfolds, just
one concentric womb en route to another,
each encompassing the last; the labor
before us, our tunnel to the future;
the film covering our eyes, torn
away slowly, as we form inwardly,
no longer able to pretend.

SURVIVING HAS
MADE ME CRAZY

I eat flowers now and birds follow me.
I open myself like an inlet
and dolphin-like energies
swim on through.

Wherever I go, I remain silent
and the silence begins to glow
till one eye in the light
outsees two in the dark.

When asked, I now hesitate,
for there are so many ways
to love the earth.

I water things now constantly:
water the hearts of dead friends with light,
the sores of the living with anything warm,
water the skies with a thousand affections
and follow the voices of animals
into grasses that move like ocean.

I eat flowers now and birds come.
I eat care and things to love arrive.
I eat time and as I age
whatever I swallow grows timeless.

I eat and undie
and water my doubts
with silence
and birds come.

FOR THAT

How could I know
creating and surviving
were so close

a membrane apart,
a pulsing, glowing film

of will, the muscle;
faith, the will
flexed.

How could I know
each day
is
the last
and
the first

and beneath
that tension,
if we wade below it
like the surface
of a sea, a chance
only coral
can feel

and there
we grow
so thoroughly

that breaking
and healing,
creating
and surviving,
first and
last are
one, the
same.

There,
beneath
the tensions
of psychology,
beneath the
pockets of doubt,
beneath the
prospect of
days to be lived
or not lived,

a moment
so calm

it is
cleansing

and I smile
through my
whole body
just to have
a body,
just to have

this orchestra
within that plays
to no conductor.

Will you believe me then,
that like the Zen monk
who finds wisdom
in his fears,
who hears more
than he can say,

will you believe me
that no matter what
is shucked or diagnosed
or bled, I would
trade places
with no one,
spirits
with all.

My purpose,
at last,
to hold
nothing
back.

My goal:
to live
a thousand years,
not in succession,
but in every
breath.

Questions to Walk With

- In your journal, describe a time when you were asked to cross a line to get involved and stop watching. What made you cross that line? What made you get involved? Where does that quality of heart live in you? Can you have a conversation with it? Can you befriend that quality of heart and take its counsel?

- Grief is such a universal and personal experience. In your journal, tell the story of someone you've lost and how their presence has appeared to you since their death.

- In conversation with a friend or loved one, describe a time when the voice inside you changed its language and how you came to understand its new way of speaking. What has the voice inside been saying to you lately?

- We are drawn to follow what matters. In conversation with a friend or loved one, describe three ways that what matters has appeared to you. What have these experiences shown you about the nature of what matters and how you relate to it?

- In conversation with a friend or loved one, describe your experience of aging. What do you feel opening as you live longer?

- In your journal, describe one aspect of your life that you would not trade with anyone and why. How does this aspect give you strength? How do you access it during times of stress and fear?

FLINT WORK

A *Sufi master and his apprentice were traveling across the desert to
a marketplace by the sea. Crossing the desert, the apprentice didn't
see much difference between himself and the master. To himself, the apprentice
mused, it's not as far to truth as I thought. But once in the marketplace, the
apprentice couldn't take a step clearly. He saw a beautiful woman from
afar, and he wanted to touch her, and wrestling with his desire to touch her, he
stopped experiencing her. Now he was fishing in the break of his heart, mourning
the last love he'd known, wondering where she was. Then he saw an angry
father strike his son, and everyone else kept walking by. Now he was feeling his
anger at his own father and was no longer experiencing the street. Then, beyond
the fish peddlers, a snake handler was dancing in the air, and the apprentice
was now caught in his mother's fear of snakes. When the master reached for the
young man, it was as if he were reaching through a dark fog. The apprentice
was startled. The master held his face and said, "When you can walk the city
like a desert and the desert like a city, the sun will be your heart above you and
your heart will be the sun inside you."*

Most of us live with the pressured thoughts of the apprentice
lodged between who we are and our experience of the world. That
is, our hurts, slights, questions, and discomforts build like a
dark cloud between our soul and our way in the world. It is this
natural and recurring buildup, when not released, that keeps us
from directly experiencing life. The truth is that both the master
and the apprentice are alive in each of us. The image of walking
the desert without distraction, with nothing but the sun on our
skin, is symbolic of unencumbered living. Of course, while in that
moment, the unfiltered truth of life as we meet it seems handy,
accessible, and easy to maintain.

But as soon as we enter the psycho-spiritual spheres of others,
we struggle constantly with every thought and feeling they emit and

represent. Imagine rain on a lake and each drop cross-rippling with all the others. Emotionally, we wash into each other in just this way. As the apprentice learns, the fiber of our integrity is tested more in community than in solitude. How often do we sit before another and experience their emotional reflection cross-rippling into all that we fear? How hard it is to truly experience who or what is before us, the way we experience the sun in the desert.

We all experience this buildup of perception, which, as it grows, creates a dark pocket between our spirit and our skin. Unrelieved of this, we begin to live farther from ourselves. Unrelieved of this, we begin to live smaller than we really are. This dynamic is inescapable. We're left with the need to somehow gather what we feel and know and then to somehow release its buildup. No one can escape the ever-pregnant need to soil ourselves with experience and to then cleanse the residue; again and again, soil and cleanse, experience and release—flint work of the soul.

What seems key to all this is a willingness to find new ways to bleed what Carl Jung calls our shadow, that is, the buildup of that dark cloud of repressed feeling we all carry.

As we struggle with all we carry, we discover that what is not *ex-pressed* is *de-pressed*. It seems the more we express, that is bring out what is in, the more alive we are. The more we give voice to our pain in living, the less buildup we have and so, our inner life fits our outer life more fully.

The more we depress, the more we push down and keep in, the smaller we become. The more we stuff between our heart and our daily experience, the more we have to work through to feel the directness of authentic living. Our unexpressed life can become a callous or bark we carry around and manicure but never remove. And so, unexpressed experience can insulate us from the essential tenderness and poignancy of life, as we mistakenly conclude that life is losing its meaning. To a man unaware of the cataracts filming his eyes, the world seems dimmer, not his seeing. How often do we find the world less stimulating, unaware that our heart is diminished because of its encasement in all that remains unexpressed?

In moments of being unencumbered, we are congruent, and the body fits the soul like a glove. It's important to note that to express, to bring what is in out, is not limited to the act of being verbal. Expressing includes any act of embodiment, be it dancing, singing, drumming, or praying silently. It includes manifesting one's inwardness just as cleanly in solitude as in the presence of others. In truth, all these forms of expression—gestural and verbal, alone and with others—are essential.

Let me give a personal example. I have, for many reasons, including issues of my own making, forever felt invisible in family or group settings. Initially, this stemmed from fearfully pleasing a narcissistic mother at all cost. It led to years of unexpressed hurts and rejections, which accrued into a callous that guarded the heart within my heart. I am and have always been a very open and emotionally accessible person, but at a certain depth, the surviving core could not be touched. Though this started with mother, I cultivated this protection, and it affected the depth at which I could relate to anyone.

Eventually, this didn't work. It wasn't enough. I realized the world was not losing color, but that I was screening the deepest emotional colors out. That I state this so calmly and clearly in one sentence hardly reflects the difficult and slow, grinding way this awareness pained itself into my daily consciousness. Rather, it emerged in me gradually as I began to acknowledge and voice the hurts and feelings of invisibility I've carried all my life.

In feeling safe enough to say this or that hurt me—to myself or to a therapist or a loved one—I inherently affirmed my emotional existence in two ways. First, in expressing these pains, I, for the first

185

time, affirmed that I have feelings to be hurt. Secondly, by clearly accepting and attesting that others have hurt me, I established that I am not solely responsible for all the pain I've experienced. In essence, expressing what was hidden gave me proof that I exist with a right to the emotional life inherent in being human.

As these repressed pains found their way like bubbles to the surface, insights of acceptance were seeping through to the heart within my heart. By ex-pressing, I was releasing some of the pressurized thoughts of the apprentice. I was beginning to free myself from the noise of the marketplace.

During this time, I couldn't trust the extent of my reactions. For instance, when first separated from a marriage of twenty years, some of my closest friends exiled me. One couple in particular was reminiscent of my parents. One partner was vocal and maintained the foreground, while the other was somewhat reticent, adaptive in the background. When they spurned me, I was deeply hurt. The more vocal of the two took the lead, but I became enraged more deeply with the reticent partner. Though I was wounded, I felt that my reaction was out of proportion to what happened. Over time, I realized I was angry that the reticent partner didn't voice her own feelings or take her own stand in all of this.

Slowly, it became clear that she reminded me of my own reticence over the years. I was angry at myself as well. It also became clear that she was hiding behind her partner, the way my father always hid behind my domineering mother. Even when my parents would write, my mother would speak for both of them and even sign his name. Through the rejection of my friends, I was finally ex-pressing the legacy of hurt from all those years of my father never taking a stand or voicing his love directly, as well as the pain of my own silence along the way.

When another lifelong friend balked at helping me move for fear of offending my former wife, I felt discarded. Finally, after several months, I told him how I felt. It was awkward, and we both were afraid how this would affect our friendship. I realized, only later, that I was looking for him to say he was sorry, which he did, though not using those words. I was angry with him, again somewhat out of proportion to what happened. It came to me later that in all my years on Earth, I've never heard my mother say she is sorry for anything. Not once.

Through what my friends incurred and what they happened to trigger within me, I released a great deal of shadow buildup and the callous around my inner heart became more porous. These are just two examples of a myriad of de-pressed feelings I've carried since childhood that I am still in the process of releasing. Miraculously, yet not surprisingly, I am finding that, on the other side of giving voice to these pains, I am closer to my skin, closer to the air I breathe, closer to the words I speak and hear, closer to tears than ever. The water within is more on the surface.

Whatever your own example, it seems our authenticity is tied to what is de-pressed and what is ex-pressed. Just as flowers need healthy roots in order to blossom, feelings can only express their beauty when rooted cleanly within us. Then they can break ground and sprout outside us. It is that delicate paradoxical inch of ground between surface and depth, between flower and root, between what is allowed out and what is allowed in that continually determines whether we are living our lives or not.

Jesus said, "The eye is the lamp of the body. If your eye is sound, your whole body will be full of light." This implies that the eye that is clear lets light *in*. Considering the eye as something that lets light in and not just something that observes light outside itself opens the heart of the matter. In truth, considering the heart as something that lets the reality of others in and not just something that projects its desires and fears on others ushers us into the realm of risk. And risk—to let others in as well as to let ourselves out—seems essential in releasing the interior buildup of pain and its unexpressed conclusions.

One crippling duality falsely maintained in our psychology is the seeming tension between risk and safety. These two states are traditionally cast as mutually exclusive synonyms for carelessness and guardedness, where risking openness is seen as a dangerous way to lose all safety, and where keeping closed is seen as a protective way to stay safe. This reflects a wall-in-wall-out sense of being in the world. Within the wall is safe. Outside the wall is not. This, of course, never acknowledges the suffocating dangers of the wall itself.

In true interior ways, the only path to deep safety, that sea of inner peace, is through the continual surf of risk. Inwardly, risk *opens* safety. It doesn't shut it down. Only through the risk to open can we inhabit the strength and fullness of what is Whole. This raises the very profound interior question of how to define self-protection. Is it hiding who and what you are, or is it being who and what you are?

~ ~ ~

While the master sought out an old friend, the apprentice, shaken by the voices not his own, wandered the marketplace, and sat in a corner behind a woman who sold birds. She noticed but wasn't bothered by him. As the sun shifted across the open sky, the shadow of a brilliant bird and its cage silhouetted his face so that the bird seemed perched between his eyes in the cage of his head. The apprentice didn't know this, though he couldn't help but be smitten with the brilliant soft bird. When he focused on the bird, there seemed no cage, for being this bird, where else was there to go? When he focused on the bars, the world turned oppressive.

How often we walk about with the soft brilliant bird trapped in our head, without even knowing. Of course, we each must ask, what constitutes those bars, which, focused on, turn the world oppressive? What makes up the cage though we can't see it—worry, fear, doubt, anger, lack of self-worth, a refusal to accept things as they are, the urgent need for approval, a relentless fear of death—What? Even more crucial, what is the soft and brilliant bird perched between our eyes? Is it the Atman that Hindus praise, the breath of the Eternal Self exhaling from our deepest almost unreachable Center? And what must we do to see the world from that soft bird's eye? Isn't this tiny feathery spirit that lives within us worthy of our friendship?

The American poet Theodore Roethke calls this tiny voice "a light breather . . . a music in a hood," and Rilke has captured the torture of life focused only on the bars in his famous poem "The Panther":

> His vision, from the constantly passing bars,
> has grown so weary that it cannot hold
> anything else. It seems to him there are
> a thousand bars; and behind the bars, no world.

Yet like so many of life's deepest truths, we seldom experience our gifts and trials separately. A profound treatment of all this is René Magritte's eerie painting of a faceless man whose chest is an open cage with a white bird perched peacefully in the cage, not flying, though the cage remains open.

If we can see the white bird perched in its open cage as our inner heart facing the world, we are left with this quandary: Is the bird free at last and incapable of exercising its long-awaited freedom? Or, finally seeing with the eyes of inner freedom, is the bird surprised that there is nowhere to go; that what was a cage for so long is really its nest, its home; that freedom is in the heart's eye all along?

We're brought back to risk, to the question of how to protect ourselves by being who we are. We are so steeped in skepticism and distrust in our age that this simple truism might seem like an outright contradiction. In his poem, "Self-Protection," D. H. Lawrence affirms the power and durability of living by our own light when he declares that creatures that hide their essential nature have all become extinct and only those who live in outright splendor like the tiger and the nightingale have survived:

> A nightingale singing at the top of his voice
> Is neither hiding himself nor preserving himself;
> He is giving himself away in every sense of the word;
> And obviously, it is the culminating point of his
> existence . . .

A personal example of this oscillation between cage and bird is what I felt in the throes of my cancer experience. In moments of fear my illness became the oppressive bars of my cage. But inexplicably, I was somehow thrust deeper into the freedom of my inner heart, where I realized, like Magritte's white bird, that despite my fear, there was nowhere else to go—illness and all. This life was and is my nest, my home. From that feathery spirit's perch between my eyes, other psychological bars dropped from view. The urgency of my illness—the sudden prospect of not existing anymore—made visible my luxuries of denial and projection and procrastinating, and my need to sing and give myself away, no matter how softly, became ever-present, opening *Now*.

The song, to my surprise, even when no one else could hear it, began to melt the bars, and those that didn't melt split and sagged and reformed into the bent branches of my life. Amazing and mysterious yet true—the bird, if allowed to sing, shapes its tree.

Now that I am well—my cage door blown open, my cage bars now revealed as the forest I have come from—all moments of living, no matter how difficult, come back into me, into some central point that opens like that unseeable eye that Jesus speaks of. Now light pours in and out at once, and I realize that this moment, whatever it might be, is a fine moment to live and a fine moment to die.

Full of light, everything happens at once—not pain-free, but unencumbered. I'm surprised to discover that loving yourself is like feeding a clear bird no one else can see. You must be still and offer your palmful of secrets like delicate seed. As she eats your secrets, no longer secret, she glows and you lighten and her voice, which only you can hear, is your voice bereft of plans. And the light through her body will bathe you till you wonder why the gems in your palm were ever fisted. Others will think you crazed to wait on something no one sees. But the clear bird only wants to feed and fly and sing. She only wants light in her belly. And once in a great while, if someone loves you enough, they might see her rise from the nest beneath your fear.

~ ~ ~

By the time the master found the apprentice, the young man was paralyzed by his own considerations. The master had expected as much. When he saw how fixed the apprentice was on the soft brilliant bird, he beseeched the woman to let the young man hold it. At first, the bird was jittery, but the master showed the apprentice how to gently rub its head and the bird began to coo. The master crouched down, facing the young man, their eyes fixed on each other, the small soft bird between them. The master whispered, "You are the master, and I am the bird. You must hold us in view and live."

As difficult as it is to accept that there are no answers in life, it's even more difficult at times to accept that no one holds what we presume are the answers. No one. We are, unto ourselves, both master and apprentice. There is only, it seems, the returning glimpse of clarity in which all is seen and felt and the muddled aftermath when all speech fails.

In essence, as we must blink a thousand times a day, what is human in us blinks continually over our being. For if the deepest eye is that Eternal Self, then our blinking lid is the smaller self, the thin membrane of our psychology, the buildup of perception and our all-too-human need to rest. In this way, our limitations humble us, covering our gifts repeatedly. As our limitations

The Therapist by René Magritte

blink away, the thin bars around the soft brilliant bird are there then not, there then not. There is no escaping the mix of all this. There is only holding the mystery of truth in view, even when we're dark.

So what are we left with? Each of us with the endless and repeatable task of discovering, un-covering, our *enthusiasm*, which means *being at one with the energy of God or the Divine*, from the Greek *en (one with)* and *theos (the divine)*. Despite our endless limitations, it seems that the qualities of attention, risk, and compassion allow us to be at one with the energy of the Whole, and the *result* is enthusiasm. As such, enthusiasm is not a mood that can be willed or forced, but only manifest by our immersion into the current of life.

Like a bird gliding with the current of air it can't see, or a fish swimming with the tide of deep it can't see, or a note being sung as part of a song it can't see, we're all left with the necessary risk to express our demons so that the unseeable music of being may rise and carry us along. In recurring humility, our enthusiasm, our momentary oneness with the energy of the Universe, is the sound of God moving through the harp of the soul.

I recently had a moment of enthusiasm . . .

I am running. It is the end of winter, and I am running through crowds along wet city streets, feeling small, the noise of others in my head. Things that are dead are preparing against all will to come alive. Including me. I am running and see part of myself in some ice melting. There I am, by turns troubled and free, breathing heavy, like a hungry deer. Suddenly, I'm distracted by a sliver of wind rattling through cars and bodies along the glass of some store. I'm stopped by my reflection. It makes me look at myself, look through myself. I feel naked despite my gear. Feel naked despite my mind. Naked despite my strife in the world. I see myself and, for the first time, I'm not a little boy peering out of a big man's body. For the moment, I am the bird and the cage is open. Cars honk, people pass, salesmen sell. The wind rattles. For the moment,

I am staring at my Self, complete with no gaps between my soul and my life. For the moment, the cage has turned into my life, and spirit is the underside of skin, experience, the skin of spirit. The marketplace is buzzing. The deep air moves in and out. It is the same air. Inside, the air turns to feeling; outside, the air turns to thought. On my lips it is moist, an eternal condensation. I lick my lips and smile . . .

It is a mysterious and strenuous practice: to walk the city like a desert, to bleed the dark cloud that builds within us, to ex-press what is de-pressed, to let the light in. Despite all our blinking, the most crucial challenge of being human is to sing the cage into a nest.

ENTERING OUR TENTH YEAR
(For Susan)

When I say I love you, I mean that,
being near you, something opens in me
and I become a shore and not a bottle.

When I say I am lost, I mean that
the few maps I've found or made up
have brought me to the edge of the unknown.

When I say I need you, I mean that
in the way that plants need sun or earth.

When I say I am alone, I mean this
in the way that a hawk is alone in its sky.

When I can't speak at all, I don't mean
anything. It's just that I've unstitched
the words and have slipped into the
silence they contain. And there,
I find you.

COMING OF AGE

The bent trees told him
that the years will humble
and this is not to be feared.

The hummingbird sucking
nectar while working so hard
to stay aloft told him that effort
and grace are two sides of the
same moment and this is not
to be feared.

The sea wearing the cliff and
the cliff accepting the sea told him
that to smooth and be smoothed
is the covenant of love.

AFTER MIRA

One day, we think we dare to love
but find we've already given our heart
and have no choice but to work our fingers
in that unexpected garden. And unimaginable
things grow. However long the entwining of
aliveness lasts, we feel blessed, like the one
dragonfly allowed to light on the one lily pad
floating on the one calm patch of lake. And
in some moment below all we've been
taught, we know Heaven is wherever the
heart gives itself away. Then, after what
seems a lifetime and always too soon, what
we love dies or goes away and the tectonic
plates on which our life stands heave and
break and the heart we so freely gave, now
entangled with the world, is ripped apart.
Nothing makes sense while in this re-
arranging pain. Nothing. No matter what
others say, nothing is of comfort while
the heart is reforged in the furnace no
one asks for. Under it all, some infinite
part of us knows that this too, painful as
it is, is the inexplicable continuance of love:
how fires become the bed of seeds yet to be
sown, how mountains crumble into valleys,
how lovers are stilled into their wisdom,
how those who reach for the stars become
their own light. Against our will, our heart

is remade by the angel of grief who grips
the center of our life, shaking everything
dead within us from our branches, until
the heart condenses to a diamond.
Hard as this is to endure,
this too is a miracle.

STILL

After so much pain,
I still want to be here,
the way a minnow tossed
in a puddle wakes and
flips itself silly.

Somehow we go on,
loss after loss, like seeds
drowning in their possibility
under all that snow.

From a distance, stars
are pins of light pushing
back the dark.

But inside, each
is a *world* of light.

And the Spirit we carry—
that carries us—flares like a
star, everywhere we go, push-
ing back the pain and loss.

Still, a star can't be seen
without its covering of night,
nor a soul without its
human skin.

I don't know why.

It has nothing to do with
optimism and pessimism
or with triumph and defeat.

More, the irrepressible reach
of a beam of light entering the
darkest place it can find, because
that is how it fulfills itself.

How we take turns, as the star
and the dark place, how we
complete each other.

WHAT CAN I DO?

I was surprised when John,
who helped save my life, came
down with liver cancer. He had
no interest in going through this
the way I did. He didn't want to
talk. He just stared at me for hours.
I so wanted to be there for him. All
I could do was sit with him in silence.
I read books while he slept, held his
hand, tried to slow his breathing when
he was agitated. All this to say, keep
your friend company the best you can.
Give your heart to what you sense
brings her relief. If she likes to be
with dogs, be with dogs. If she likes
to smell lavender, smell lavender. If
she likes to watch The Iron Chef,
watch The Iron Chef. Ask gentle
questions, expecting nothing. Listen
for her remaining aliveness. Mist
those tender roots with time, the
one thing she doesn't have. Love
her into some small adventure
the two of you can enter, like
chasing light or watching the
first silent film. To be a second
self is a vaccine against despair.

LOVE YOUR WINDOW

No matter how small or old. Keep it
clean so you can see what comes your way.
When the lost bird flies into it looking for
its mate, keep the feather stuck to the glass.
Take it with you and dream of finding what
completes you. At the edge of winter, open
the window of your heart and see your
breath, how what you bring up becomes
the air. When you're ready or pushed,
close your eyes and the other window
will appear, the one that faces all of
time. What flies there never lands, but
hovers, dropping seeds of infinity in the
breaks we can't heal. So open the window
of your pain, though the whisperers tell you
to nail it shut, and let in everything that's
ever lived. What flies and never lands has
been waiting. Be brave. Don't run. Let the
fire around your window burn until you
become the opening.

HOURGLASS

While you were here, life seemed endless.
Now you're gone and I'm listening to Keith
Jarrett. A tune I return to when something too
beautiful or hard to bear overcomes me. A piece
on piano I always wanted you to hear. But you
never cared for music and now the thing too
beautiful and hard to bear is your death. Oh
Dad, this is all so new. I felt your absence for
years while you were alive, only to feel your
presence now, so powerful since you're gone.
Everyone is trying to remember you when you
were young, just home from the Navy, a swagger
like James Dean. But we didn't really meet until
you were ninety and I said I wanted to see you,
and you dropped the phone and began to weep.
I thought you were beautiful in the worn shell of
your body, beautiful as you took my hand when
you could no longer speak. There were so many
places I wanted to take you: the harbor in South
Africa, the docks of Sausalito, the Jewish Ceme-
tery in Prague. You never understood me, but a
whole life of trying, worth the few moments we
tripped into the bottom of things. And though
you died while I was in the air, I felt you push
your raft away from shore, felt the gentleness
of the water you so loved surround you, can feel
it now. I wanted so much to tell you of the sea I
found, the one that found me, to tell you how

I was asked to let go of all that defined me, in-
cluding you, in order to discover what matters.
Oh Dad, this descent into the heart where I
finally held your face in the hospital when
everyone went home—a deep part of who
you were left you to give me life, and I
gave it back to you, so you could die.

Questions to Walk With

- In your journal, describe what it means to you to be humble. Tell the story of a time when life humbled you and what that experience opened.

- In conversation with a friend or loved one, discuss what it means to you to have a covenant with love. What does it mean to you to be loving, and what does that look like in how you live your days?

- In conversation with a friend or loved one, describe the simplest thing someone has ever done for you and how it touched you. Then, imagine the simplest thing you can do for someone in the days ahead.

- In conversation with a friend or loved one, describe your favorite window: where it is, the first time you came upon it, why it is your favorite, and what it has shown you. Then describe the kind of window you are and what others might see through you.

- In your journal, describe the things you need to make you more whole-hearted and more of a complete human being. Try to be specific and name the places you need to go, the people you need to meet, the experiences you need to have in order to encounter the things that might complete you.

- We have traveled through great depths on this journey. In this final invitation, I invite you to explore—in your journal and then in conversation with a friend or loved one—one resource you need to gain strength from in order to endure suffering, as well as one aspect of your soul you need to be intimate with in order to approach wholeness, and one way that you are still here, still wondering.

THE BRIDGE OF WELL-BEING

Whether conscious of it or not, we are all engaged in the search for the unknown other who might complete us and join us to the Whole. Our longing to join and come alive is our birthright. And similar to pollination, we complete the world when, opening ourselves against great odds, some strange unknown partner inadvertently seeds our essence elsewhere.

My interest in this surfaced twenty years ago with a dream. I was walking across a very old and rickety bridge, one that had been repaired generation after generation, and as I neared the middle, a young man, reverberating in his own inner turmoil, jumped into the fast-moving river below. I was panicked and ran off the bridge and down the bank where medics were on the scene, except instead of a physician, an Asian sage, barefoot and bearded, was suddenly beside me. As they were dragging the young man's body to us—he was waterlogged and broken—I looked to the sage who appeared unalarmed. He registered the concern on my face, took me by the arm, and said, "It happens all the time." I asked, "What was he after?" "Oh," shrugged the sage, "he was searching for *the fellow*. He thought he saw it calling him in the water. It happens all the time."

I had no idea at the time, but this dream was a myth about enduring suffering and approaching wholeness. I had no idea that this dream was a parable of my journey through cancer. When I jumped into the river of life so long ago, I was looking for the unknown other that would complete me. I thought I would find wholeness through love or passion for some kind of work or in the depth of my creativity. I had no idea that the thing that would complete me was being broken open by cancer.

Inevitably, we are all searching for the fellow—the other, the stranger, the conduit, living or not, sentient or not—the repeatable and varied bridge that might join us to ourselves and thereby to the Whole of God's Being. *Fellow,* from the Old Norse meaning *partner, one who lays down wealth.* And the word *wealth* is from the Middle English *welthe* meaning originally *well-being.* *Fellow, one who lays down his well-being,* not laying down in the sense of giving up or relinquishing one's true nature, but rather in the sense of unfolding or opening the way between living things. And so we are all searching—outwardly or inwardly—for the bridge of well-being, wherever we might find it. Why? Because in moments of being bridged, we not only actualize ourselves but simultaneously are in accord with the Universe—we briefly *become* the Universe—the way it's impossible in a tree erect with wind to separate its leaves from the air.

One of the great paradoxes of being is that each of us is born complete and yet we need contact with life in order to be whole. This, then, is the purpose of the stranger: to enliven what is dormant within us. Once enlivened, it is our responsibility to keep what's dormant conscious and to integrate the fibers of hard-earned experience into the fabric of a living spirit.

The word *stranger* denotes a living embodiment of that which is strange. But the word strange means more than being odd and unfamiliar. The word *strange* comes from the Old French, *estrange,* which means *extraordinary.* Ultimately, the stranger functions as an unexpected messenger who can embody or mirror what is extraordinary within us, what is possible but yet unlived.

The strange messenger is an extraordinary completing agent that disrupts what is familiar in order that we might grow; sometimes by mending us and sometimes by breaking down our walls. And whether it be someone who finally loves you for who you are or a fire that destroys all your paintings or the sudden appearance of a deer staring at you in the wet snow, the strange messenger serves as a catalyst that opens us to a deeper way of living. Whether embodied in an event or in a person or in a break in our comfortable way of thinking, experiencing the extraordinary brings us closer to the ongoing Unity of Creation of which we all are a part.

The strange messenger can arrive as a cloud or a brick: as a lyric of truth piped over your head in a restaurant, drifting into the center of all your confusion at just the right instant, or as a sudden wind that relieves you of a certain map, forcing you to find your way by other means. But inevitably, the presence of the extraordinary, whether harsh or kind, will reconnect us with the rest of the Universe.

In the twenty years since having this dream, I've been visited by many strange messengers, and each has been a bridge that has brought me closer to life. Each has turned me inside out in a way that has revealed the extraordinary waiting in the ordinary. Of course, there was my cancer. But there was, as well, my wheeling of Grandma Minnie into the sun in the courtyard of Kingsbrook Medical Center in Brooklyn, just months before she died. And the way Ann and Robert and I helped save each other's lives. And the mysterious bridge by which Robert and I have stayed friends and Ann and I have not. And for my wife Susan and me, there was the strange messenger that was Mira, our furry dog-child who was a wordless angel for thirteen years. Mira bridged me more deeply into nature where I met my older self. And the blessed strange messengers that have been my books, teachers leading me across many canyons into a more wakeful life. And the long, delicate bridge that I have traveled with Susan, so real and sweet and long that the bridge itself has become a home.

No matter how young or old, how innocent or experienced, we all long for the bridge of well-being that will complete us.

When touched by a strange messenger that arrives in the form of a person, a powerful relationship unfolds, and we often start to mistake the messenger for the message. Despite the mix of lessons and blessings that lead us to what lives within us, we tend to imbue the stranger as extraordinary. We're so happy to be seen that we're pulled into the magnetism of desire, empowering the stranger with the key to what has been growing quietly within us all along. If we never claim the light in our heart, we start to believe that the energy of life is other than where we are. This is the seed of unworthiness, for now we believe that we need the stranger, when it is the message of the extraordinary we can't live without.

It's taken me years to understand that there's a fire in each of us that we steward and the gift of every true relationship is that it fans our inner flame, which, once known to us, we must tend ourselves and keep going. So often, we inflate and overempower those we love; somehow convinced *they* are the source of our newfound spot of flame.

A very common example of this is the urgency of first love. A woman's inner mind is taken seriously for the first time by a gentle lover, and she is frightened to live without him, for fear he is the only one that can unlock her deepest thoughts. A rock of a man is made safe and therefore softens in the arms of a certain woman, and he can't let her out of his sight, terrified that without her touch he'll turn back to stone. I was no different. I remember my first love and how alive I felt. Bearing witness to my tiny budding self, she mirrored my own goodness, which I attributed completely to her. I ached for her with an urgency, believing she carried the goodness I feared I'd never find.

Very often, that initial stirring of our ability to feel is so full of wonder and pain that we think it is beyond us. And overwhelmed, we begin to believe that this sudden awakening to the depth of life is within the power of the loved one to bestow or withhold.

The pangs of attachment are severe enough without enshrining a loved one as the gatekeeper of our newly discovered passion. The highest tribute we can pay a loved one is to own what they have awakened in us and nurture it. In doing so, we become more capable of love, and more capable of honoring that loved one for who they truly are, without keeping them on a pedestal. After my first love moved on, it took ten years for the pedestal I'd created for her to erode. And slowly, as I met other strange messengers, as I crossed other bridges of well-being, I began to meet the world rather than hide from it. I began to enter life rather than sort and rank the living.

Often, our passion for a particular way of being is driven by others into a grand goal of becoming, as if life doesn't reside in who we are but only in the dream of what we might become. In the same way that the loved one can be seen as the keeper of our gift, our idealized ambition—becoming a rock star or a famous writer or a celebrated photographer—can be seen as the keeper of a role that will let us truly live, if we can just reach it. In this way, we misconstrue what is ever-present within us as some far-off possibility. In this way, we become dependent on our ambition to define us rather than our true nature.

It's fine to work toward goals, as long as we believe in the work and resist deifying the goals. When our life-force appears as a passion that we put off inhabiting by hiding it in some future ambition or goal, we stall our growth. And without our knowing, the joy of singing is distilled into a dream of being recorded. The transformation of writing is condensed into a need to be published. A love of seeing, manifest through painting or photography, is inverted into a need to be seen.

Like so many young writers, I thought that being published would validate my identity in some idealized future. I was secretly desperate to be seen by others, when I really needed to see myself and feel where my soul joins with the rest of life. I was full of misplaced labor. But thankfully, life has many strange messengers to reduce us to who we are. Thankfully, there are many unexpected bridges that bring us humbly to where we are.

Like it or not, we are drawn to the form of fellow or stranger we need. Most of us pursue that impulse as a hobby, never taking the risk to make completeness our vocation. So an insurance man who skydives on weekends is searching for the fellow, which in him takes the form of the need to fall with no control and the need at the last second to save himself with one sure gesture. Yet, it is not the feeding of that need that will save his life, but the search for where that need begins. For acting out the need will often destroy us, while uncovering its source will often preserve us.

Consider the alcoholic who seeks his strange messenger in a bottle, always trying to fill an ever-growing thirst. Here, acting out the need often leads to death, for the source of the thirst is a spiritual emptiness, which drink does not satisfy but deadens. The reason Alcoholics Anonymous has been so astonishing in its success is that it provides painfully empty spirits with the search for the fellow—the other in themselves and in those around them, a search that can join them to the Whole. AA offers people who are broken open a bridge of well-being to God and to each other.

The alcoholic is not alone. We all need a bridge to an otherness that will enliven us. The mechanic, who feeds his family by fixing what others break, takes up scuba diving, the fellow in him needing to breathe beneath the surface. And some search at daybreak watching quietly for rare birds, secretly wanting the simplicity of beak and wing and branch, while others inhabit their solitude, searching the edge of who they are for the threshold of all they are not.

Our search for Wholeness is both inward and outward, into the core of our own existence and into the life of others—be they breathing others, panting others, or flowering others. All in search of a way to join with all of life.

This need to uncover what we have in common with all life constitutes a different form of salvation, not a removal from the earthly as monasticism or asceticism would offer and not an absolution from mistakes as Christianity would have it, but salvation as the self-actualization that removes whatever exists between our daily life and the pulse of being that is the Heartbeat of the Universe.

Thomas Merton describes our search for the unknown other who might complete us in *this* life as

> the full discovery of who (we) really (are) . . . the fulfillment of (our) own God-given powers . . . (and) the discovery that (we) cannot find (ourselves) in (ourselves) alone, but that (we) must find (ourselves) in and through others.

Earlier, I shared that in wheeling Ann to surgery, I could only wheel her so far, and waiting there at the door of the operating room, I realized that no one can go beyond the glass door with you. There is no question that, for me, in that moment, the glass door became the stranger, the messenger of the extraordinary. And very often, the person escorting us to and from the glass door is our completing other. Indeed, the most powerful form of messenger is the unexpected presence of a loved one. Why? Because through their love, we often see what we are capable of but not living, and this unnerves us at our core. So the bottom gets stirred up, which is painful and confusing, but all of us comes alive.

It seems that difficulty is woven into the design of life, so that we need the presence of others to help us through and bring each other alive. The bridge of our well-being is often made visible when the stranger, the fellow, the completing other jars us to inhabit our life. During the last few years, I have been jarred alive by the silence of a friend as we hiked up a mountain at sunrise with her dogs. And I was yoked into the unnamed center of my soul when holding my father's hand, as he slept in a wheelchair months before his death. And just last week, I was stopped by the twilight as it made the skeleton of a tree dance without moving.

Throughout this book, we have explored this truth from many vantage points: that the gift of true relationship is that we awaken and complete each other. This is a very ancient and vibrant idea. In Greek mythology it's believed that only when the Gods vanish or die, can humans have interior fire. Indeed, it's believed that a function of the death of a great spirit is that its fire will then ignite within the hearts of those remaining. The loss of a loved one *is* such a piece of God, a form of Spirit whose coming and going draws us more rawly into the open. Having done so, the piece of God vanishes and we are hurtled into the pain of grief and loss. The very covenant of legacy is that what we loved in those who died is now ours to keep alive.

I feel this so deeply with the death of my father. Though we were so different in the world, we were at heart the same. And now, when I touch something he carved out of wood, when I hold the chisel he used for half a century, I feel the creative fire he left growing in me. And the legacy of a friend I loved who died of cancer is that I feel her fierce honesty awakening in me. Such is the power of true relationship. As the eighteenth-century philosopher Saint-Martin remarks, "My friends are the beings through whom God loves me."

Can it be that when we join by daring to open the way between all living things, we piece the broken world back together?

~ ~ ~

Since I first had that dream twenty years ago of the young man jumping off a bridge in search of the fellow, I have been fascinated with bridges. For they always uphold the endless story of how we help each other from one point of aliveness to the next. And there's one bridge in particular that speaks to the journey from suffering to wholeness. It is *The Suspension Bridge Between Hida and Etchu*, a woodblock print by the Japanese Master Hokusai (1760–1849). He carved and printed this in the early 1830s. In the scene, two travelers, carrying their belongings, carefully balance their way across a thin, ropelike bridge. The bridge crosses a small ravine, so high that it sways among the clouds. It's unclear where

The Suspension Bridge Between Hida and Etchu by Hokusai

215

these travelers are going or coming from. The entire focus of the woodblock is where each traveler steps. The whole world seems to bend to the point of their steps.

I share this because it captures the power and poignancy of our time on Earth. We have to go from here to there, but the life—the aliveness we treasure, the company that matters—is always in the tenderness of each step. It is in each step that we find ourselves and each other. It is in each step that we hold each other up.

It remains a powerful mystery that when I look deeply enough into you, I find me, and when you dare to hear my fear in the recess of your heart, you recognize it as your secret which you thought no one else knew. And that unexpected Wholeness that is more than each of us, but common to all—that moment of unity is the atom of God.

ADRIFT

Everything is beautiful and I am so sad.
This is how the heart makes a duet of
wonder and grief. The light spraying
through the lace of the fern is as delicate
as the fibers of memory forming their web
around the knot in my throat. The breeze
makes the birds move from branch to branch
as this ache makes me look for those I've lost
in the next room, in the next song, in the laugh
of the next stranger. In the very center, under
it all, what we have that no one can take
away and all that we've lost face each other.
It is there that I'm adrift, feeling punctured
by a holiness that exists inside everything.
I am so sad and everything is beautiful.

THE BEAUTY
OF LESS

We think to get what
we want is our destiny.
But to reach and miss
lets us land where we are.
This is the maturing of our
destiny. And landing there
lets the light in each moment
emanate like the sun. Holding
stones and pain and each other
in this light turns ambition
into being. The beauty of less
lets the seed of everything
sprout within us.

Between the Wall
and the Flame

You ask, "How can you believe in
anything when there's pain everywhere?"
And I see the pain in your face. I have no
answer, anymore than day can make its case
in the middle of the night. Yes, things are
breaking constantly and people, bent from
their nature, are cruel and our desperation
leads us to an excess that is even too heavy
for the planet to bear. Yet, I am in a wine
bar in Hell's Kitchen, against a brick wall,
and the small flame from the oil lamp is
letting the wall whisper its long history.
And somehow in the lighted inch of
brick, what matters flickers and I feel
everything. Something between the wall
and the flame flutters like a butterfly
carrying the secret of peace, unseen,
unnoticed. And even seeing it, and
feeling it briefly, I don't know how to
speak of it. It's as if under the earthquake
of existence, an infinite hand holds the
ball of fire that is our world. Now some-
one nearby pokes me and asks, "So, are
you talking about God?" This is beyond
anything I have a concept for. We're like
small urchins churned over in the surf of
time. There's so much more than we can

know. But you are still hurting. So I'll
stop talking. Come, put your head
on my shoulder.

EVENTUALLY

We stop trying
to carry all that we know
as if it will protect us.

If lucky, we are forced
to accept that under
what we think is ours
is the beginning
of what no one owns.

At last, we are
humbled to dip our face
in the same well.

It is the look of your
face and mine
lifting from that well
that frees me.

THROWN BACK

Twenty-six years ago today, the tumor growing in my skull vanished, and I was thrown back in the streets like Lazarus. Today the rain is a fine mist, and I open my face for a long time, receiving water from the sky. All I can say is perhaps falling in love with the world is the bravest thing we can do. I only know that my heart grows stronger every year, a muscle gaining each time I love. This rush of life is all we have, and still we struggle to get out of it. Like fish we labor to make it to the sand as if that shore were Heaven. And when thrown back, we can grow bitter if we think we've failed or be humbled to accept that waking tomorrow in all of this *is* being saved.

THE SLOW ARM
OF ALL THAT MATTERS
(A Song for Pilgrims)

I have fallen through and worked into
a deeper way—one step at a time, one pain
at a time, one grief at a time, one amends at
a time—until the long, slow arm of all that matters
has bowed my estimation of heaven. Now, like a
heron waiting for the waters to clear, I look for
heaven on earth and wait for the turbulence to
settle. And I confess, for all the ways we stir things
up, I can see that though we can stop, life never
stops: the lonely bird crashes into the window
just as the sun disperses my favorite doubt, a
sudden wind closes your willing heart as the
moment of truth passes between us, and the
damn phone rings as my father is dying. All
these intrusions, majestically unfair, and not
of our timing. So we spin and drop and catch
and land. And sometimes, we fall onto these
little islands of stillness, like now, from which
we are renewed by our kinship with all and that
irrepressible feeling resurrects our want to be here,
to push off again into the untamable stream.

THE THIN MAGIC

We're just now climbing out of the
ravine and so the guard around my
heart is loosening and I cry easily.
Stillness is showing its face, again.
I almost lost you. Was forced to try
it on. Your roots, growing in my heart
for years, were ripped up by the storm.
We were hanging by a thread. But mir-
acle of the ordinary, hard skin graft of
time—we're still here. And light is again
whispering along the empty chairs in the
park. And pigeons sit on top of store signs
watching as we die and come alive again.
A young couple now in front of me.
They're falling into each other's future,
not knowing what ravine they will have
to cross. It would all be despairing, if not
for the thin magic of how the light from
the beginning skips through every heart
that dares to love. The barely seeable
light that slips now up the edge of
our grief, like another dawn
we're not quite ready for.

In the Sky of Heart

It's late in the afternoon and I'm
backed up in traffic, aching for my
father and our dog, both gone, when
the sun comes through, and there, above
us, a shelf of clouds shaped like an island
edged by a waterfall. So real, I can al-
most hear the rush of water falling
into Eternity. This mythic island in
the sky stands by itself, beckoning.
And I understand why early people
overwhelmed with survival might
look up and believe that gods live
in the sky. I am no different, as I
outwait the clouds of our trouble.
Someone is honking. But something
stirs within and I want to put the car
in park and walk into the sky, to sit
by the waterfall of time falling into
everything. I think it's where we all
go when the light turns green and
the tires turn to wings and the steer-
ing wheels open into flowers. I think
I hear my father throwing sticks to
our dog at the bottom of the water-
fall. Someone else is honking.
It's hard to go anywhere.

THE SWAY OF IT ALL

And so I lift my face from the mud,
the mud of my past, the mud of history,
the thick and ragged bark of how we
think everyone but our own darkness
is the enemy, I lift my face like a worn
planet spinning on itself to get back
into the light, to say to no one, to
everyone—it is an honor to be alive.

GRATITUDES

Long ago, I was lifted from almost drowning and dragged on shore, and cared for till I could walk again. Then I was gently encouraged not to fear the sea, and given stories that helped me believe there is more wonder than pain. So no matter how life has rearranged the path, no matter how scattered the tribe has become, no matter how many times I had to begin again, gratitude is all I ever have to say. There are too many to name—from the young nurse who eased me back down when the slit in my groin began to bleed to my brother who pleaded with me not to give up—there are too many to thank, each a bead of kindness on my personal rosary. And whether gone or far away, I pray for each of them. Like so many others, I was remade by the fire of life's forces and plunged into the sea of being to set the rawness and cool the burns. That's why, at a certain time of day, my inner eyes glow. That's why I feel compelled to share what I see, ever humbled by the remaking of time.

For making the earlier editions of this book possible, I am indebted to Joe Bruchac, the great Abenake poet and storyteller, and his wife, Carol, who in 1994 published the second edition with their press, Ithaca House Books. And deep thanks to my dear friend Tom Callanan who brought the former publisher of Parabola, Joe Kulin, and I together, which resulted in the first recorded edition, which was published in 1996. Tom also brought in Therese Schroeder-Sheker, a remarkable musician who has pioneered the use of voice and harp in hospice work. Tom midwifed a creative bond between the three of us, and we were off to the recording studio in New York. I must also acknowledge and thank the gracious Joe Kulin who introduced me to the intimacy of my own voice so many years ago.

And closer to the making of this book, I am grateful to my agent, Jennifer Rudolph Walsh, and the WME team for their belief and deep guidance. And to Brooke Warner for her steadfastness and care. And I'm deeply grateful for the care and excellence of the Sounds True family for preserving the heart of this work: especially to Tami Simon for her vision and love, and to my editor, Haven Iverson, and my producer, Steve Lessard, for their creative companionship.

Gratitude to the dear friends who make up my tribe. Especially George, Don, Paul, Skip, TC, David, Kurt, Pam, Patti, Karen, Paula, Ellen, Linda, Michelle, Rich, Carolyn, Henk, Sandra, Elesa, Stacy, Anders, Sally, and Joel. And to sweet Eleanor who left us too soon. And to my brother Howard for his depth of care. And to Oprah Winfrey for the immensity of her heart.

And more than I can say to Paul Bowler who put everything down to see me through. And to Robert Mason who has been my Virgil since the beginning. And to my dear wife, Susan, who has never asked me to be anything but who I am.

NOTES

Enduring Suffering

1. Anthony de Mello, *One Minute Wisdom* (New York: Doubleday, 1986).

GOD, SELF, AND MEDICINE

1. "God, Self, and Medicine" was first published in *Voices, the Journal of the American Academy of Psychotherapists* (Fall 1989, Vol. 25, No. 3). The essay also appears as a chapter in the nursing text *The Patient's Voice: Experiences of Illness,* edited by Jeanine Young-Mason (Philadelphia: F.A. Davis, 1997), 136–142.
2. A. Merriam Webster (ed.), *Webster's Seventh New Collegiate Dictionary* (Springfield, MA: G & C Merriam Company, 1972), 878.
3. Alfred Kazin (ed.), *The Portable Blake* (New York: Viking Press, 1946), 250.
4. Paul Tillich, *Dynamics of Faith* (New York: Harper and Brothers, 1957), 4.

A TERRIBLE KNOWLEDGE

1. First published in *The Journal of Pastoral Counseling* (Iona College), 1994 annual issue, pp. 153–165.
2. Aldous Huxley, *The Perennial Philosophy* (New York: Harper & Row, 1990), vii.
3. Richard Carlyon (ed.), *A Guide to the Gods* (New York: Quill Publishers, 1981), 38.
4. Joseph Campbell, *Oriental Mythology* (New York: Penguin Books, 1976), 141.
5. James G. Frazer, *Folklore of the Old Testament* (New York: Avenel Books. 1988), 26.
6. Joseph Campbell, *Oriental Mythology* (New York: Penguin Books, 1976), 139.
7. Jonathan Star (ed.), *Two Suns Rising* (New York: Bantam, 1991), 128. For purposes of our discussion, I have replaced *love's cruelty* with *life's cruelty.*

8. James G. Frazer, *Folklore of the Old Testament.* (New York: Avenel Books, 1988), 28.
9. Richard Carlyon (ed.), *A Guide to the Gods* (New York: Quill Publishers, 1981), 22.
10. Joseph Campbell, *Oriental Mythology*, 3.
11. *Mathews' Chinese-English Dictionary* (Cambridge, MA: Harvard University Press, 1960), 114.

DANCE OF THE SEED

1. First published in *Voices, the Journal of the American Academy of Psychotherapists,* Vol. 27, No. 4, Winter 1991, pp. 45–50.

APPROACHING WHOLENESS

1. Rabindranath Tagore, "Song XII," in *Gitanjali,* cited in *Critical Response to Indian Poetry in English,* by A. N. Prasad and B. Sarkar (London: Sarup & Sons, 2008), 125. Originally published 1913.

TROUBLED WATERS

1. Given as a sermon in October 1992 at the Unity Church of Albany, New York.
2. A. H. Maslow, *The Farther Reaches of Human Nature* (New York: Penguin Books, 1976), 273.
3. Linda Hess and Shukdev Singh (trans.), *The Bijak of Kabir* (San Francisco: North Point Press, 1983), 48.
4. My epic poem, "Fire Without Witness," published in Latham, NY: British American Publishing, 1988.
5. Robert Mason, *Basic Facts of Mental Life,* 1992, 17. In Manuscript. Robert's new book of poems, *Nearer to Never,* will be published by SUNY Press in spring 2016.
6. The New Testament, John, Chapter 5, "The Cure at the Pool of Bethsaida," Verses 1–13.
7. William Morris (ed.), *The American Heritage Dictionary* (Boston: Houghton Mifflin, 1978), 1520.
8. Ibid., 945.

WHO WILL LIVE YOUR LIFE?

1. First published in *Pilgrimage, Reflections on the Human Journey*, Vol. 18, No. 5, Nov./Dec. 1992, pp. 2–8.
2. Stephen Mitchell (ed.), *The Enlightened Heart* (New York: Harper & Row, 1989), 76.
3. Kenneth Rexroth (ed.), *One Hundred Poems from the Japanese* (New York: New Directions, 1964), 116.
4. Ray Charles, Proctor's Theatre, Schenectady, NY, October 16, 1991.
5. Anthony Storr, *Solitude* (New York: The Free Press, 1988), 53.
6. Thomas Merton, *New Seeds of Contemplation* (New York: New Directions, 1972), 98.
7. Anthony Storr, *Solitude*, 15
8. Burton Watso (trans.), *The Basic Writings of Chuang Tzu* (New York: Columbia University Press, 1964), 77.

CHORES

1. First published in *Pilgrimage, Reflections on the Human Journey*, Vol. 20, No. 1, Jan./Feb. 1994, pp. 25–28. A different version of this essay also appears in *The Exquisite Risk,* (New York: Harmony Books, 2005), 245.

STILL HERE, STILL WONDERING

UNRAVELING THE SELF

1. Given as a presentation at the 1999 Associated Writing Programs National Conference, Albany, NY, April 19, 1999.

SIFTING TRUTH

1. First published in *Sufi, A Journal of Sufism.* London: Khaniquahi Minatullahi Publications, Issue 47, Summer 2000.
2. Burton Watson (trans.), *Saigyo, Poems of a Mountain Home* (New York: Columbia University Press, 1991), 51.
3. Ibid., 124.
4. Robert Bly (ed.), *News of the Universe* (San Francisco: Sierra Club Books, 1980), 70.
5. Thomas Merton, *New Seeds of Contemplation* (New York: New Directions, 1961), 64.

6. Robert Bly (trans.), *Selected Poems of Rainer Maria Rilke* (New York: Harper & Row, 1981), 25.

7. John Muir, 1869, *1992 Sierra Club Calendar.*

8. Martin Büber, *Meetings.* (Chicago: Open Court Publishing, 1973), 54.

9. Burton Watson (trans.), *Basic Writings of Chuang Tzu* (New York: Columbia University Press, 1964), 59–63.

10. Thomas Cleary (trans.), *Energy, Spirit* (Boston: Shambhala, 1991), 103.

11. Ibid.

12. Rollo May, *The Courage to Create* (New York: Bantam, 1976), 61.

13. Elmer O'Brien (ed.), *Varieties of Mystical Experience* (New York: New American Library, 1965), 149.

14. Martin Büber, *Meetings,* 41–42.

15. Arthur Waley, *Three Ways of Thought in Ancient China* (New York: Macmillan, 1940), 109.

16. Burton Watson, *Saigyo, Poems of a Mountain Home* (New York: Columbia University Press, 1991), 93.

FLINT WORK

1. First published in *Sufi, A Journal of Sufism.* London: Khaniquahi Minatullahi Publications, Issue 42, Spring 1999.

2. The three italicized paragraphs about the Sufi master and his apprentice originally appeared as the story, "The Desert and the Marketplace" in my book of stories, *As Far As the Heart Can See* (Deerfield, FL: HCI Publications, 2011), 189. This essay grew out of that story.

3. Theodore Roethke, "A Light Breather" in *The Norton Anthology of Poetry,* ed. Arthur M. Eastman. (New York: Norton, 1983), 1118.

4. Stephen Mitchell (trans.), *The Selected Poetry of Rainer Maria Rilke* (New York: Vintage, 1984), 25.

5. See "The Therapist" in *Magritte,* edited by David Larkin. (New York: Ballantine Books, 1972). Originally painted in 1937.

6. Arthur M. Eastman (ed.), *The Norton Anthology of Poetry* (New York: Norton, 1983), 954.

7. This is an early version of the poem "Gemseed," which first appeared in my book *Suite for the Living,* 2004, p. 53, and which later appeared in an evolved version as the story "In the Mirror" in my book *As Far As the Heart Can See,* 2011, p. 95.

8. Anne H. Soukhanov (ed.), *American Heritage Dictionary* (Boston: Houghton Mifflin, 1992), 614.

THE BRIDGE OF WELL-BEING

1. First published in *Parabola, The Magazine of Myth and Tradition,* Volume XX, No. 2, Summer 1995, pp. 17–20. Substantially rewritten for this edition.
2. Anne H. Soukhanov (ed.), *The American Heritage Dictionary* (Boston: Houghton Mifflin, 1992), 670, 2022.
3. Ibid., 1774.
4. Thomas Merton, *No Man Is an Island* (New York: Harcourt, Brace, Jovanovich, 1955), xv.
5. Marguerite Yourcenar, *With Open Eyes: Conversations with Matthieu Galey* (Boston: Beacon Press, 1984), 260.
6. Katsushika Hokusai (1760–1849) and Utagawa Hiroshige (1797–1858) are the great woodblock print masters of Japan. Their imagination, skill, and volume of work make them the Michelangelo and Leonardo of Japanese art. *The Suspension Bridge Between Hida and Etchu,* shown here, was one of a series of bridges created in early 1830s by Hokusai (now in the Leeds Museum and Gallery, Leeds, UK).
7. This last paragraph later became part of my poem "Earth Prayer," which first appeared in my book *Suite for the Living,* 2004, p. 43.

PERMISSIONS

T hanks for permission to reprint excerpts from the following previously published works:

"God, Self, and Medicine" was first published in *Voices, the Journal of the American Academy of Psychotherapists* (Fall 1989, Vol. 25, No. 3). The essay also appears as a chapter in the nursing text *The Patient's Voice: Experiences of Illness,* edited by Jeanine Young-Mason. Philadelphia: F.A. Davis, 1997, pp. 136–142.

A prose version of "Tu Fu's Reappearance" appears as a story in my book *As Far As the Heart Can See,* HCI Publications, 2011, p. 187.

"Endgame," which also appears in my book *Suite for the Living* (Bread for the Journey, 2004), p. 70, first appeared in the original edition of *Inside the Miracle,* then titled *Acre of Light* (Ithaca House Books, 1994), p. 57.

"Endgame," "For That," "Letter Home," "Setting Fires in the Rain," "Surviving Has Made Me Crazy," and "Tu Fu's Reappearance" first appeared in *Greenfield Review Press.*

"A Terrible Knowledge" was first published in *The Journal of Pastoral Counseling* (Iona College), 1994 annual issue, pp. 153–165.

From *Masks of God: Oriental Mythology,* by Joseph Campbell, copyright © 1962 by Joseph Campbell, renewed copyright © 1990 by Jean Erdman Campbell. Used by permission of Viking Books, an imprint of Penguin Publishing Group, a division of Penguin Random House LLC.

Quotation from *The Masks of God: Oriental Mythology* by Joseph Campbell, copyright © 1962; by permission of Joseph Campbell Foundation (jfc.org).

Excerpt from *Two Suns Rising,* edited by Jonathan Star, reprinted with the permission of Jonathan Star.

"Dance of the Seed" was first published in *Voices, the Journal of the American Academy of Psychotherapists,* Vol. 27, No 4, Winter 1991, pp. 45–50.

"Troubled Waters" was given as a sermon in October, 1992 at the Unity Church of Albany, New York.

Excerpt from *The Bijak of Kabir,* translated by Linda Hess and Shukdev Singh, reprinted with the permission of Linda Hess.

"Who Will Live Your Life?" was first published in *Pilgrimage, Reflections on the Human Journey,* Vol. 18, No. 5, Nov/Dec 1992, pp. 2–8.

ABOUT THE AUTHOR

Mark Nepo moved and inspired readers and seekers all over the world with his #1 *New York Times* bestseller *The Book of Awakening.* Beloved as a poet, teacher, and storyteller, Mark has been called "one of the finest spiritual guides of our time," "a consummate storyteller," and "an eloquent spiritual teacher." His work is widely accessible and used by many, and his books have been translated into more than twenty languages. A bestselling author, he has published sixteen books and recorded eleven audio projects. Recent work includes *The Endless Practice* (Atria, 2014), cited by *Spirituality & Practice* as one of the best spiritual books of 2014; his latest book of poems, *Reduced to Joy* (Viva Editions, 2013), cited by *Spirituality & Practice* as one of the best spiritual books of 2013; a 6-CD box set of teaching conversations based on the poems in *Reduced to Joy* (Sounds True, 2014), and *Seven Thousand Ways to Listen* (Atria), which won the 2012 Books for a Better Life Award. Mark was part of Oprah Winfrey's *The Life You Want Tour* in 2014 and has appeared on her *Super Soul Sunday* program on OWN TV several times. He has also been interviewed by Robin Roberts on *Good Morning America. The Exquisite Risk* was cited by *Spirituality & Practice* as one of the best spiritual books of 2005, calling it "one of the best books we've ever read on what it takes to live an authentic life." Mark devotes his writing and teaching to the journey of inner transformation and the life of relationship. He continues to offer readings, lectures, and retreats. Please visit Mark at: MarkNepo.com, threeintentions.com, and info@wmespeakers.com.

ABOUT SOUNDS TRUE

Sounds True is a multimedia publisher whose mission is to inspire and support personal transformation and spiritual awakening. Founded in 1985 and located in Boulder, Colorado, we work with many of the leading spiritual teachers, thinkers, healers, and visionary artists of our time. We strive with every title to preserve the essential "living wisdom" of the author or artist. It is our goal to create products that not only provide information to a reader or listener, but that also embody the quality of a wisdom transmission.

For those seeking genuine transformation, Sounds True is your trusted partner. At SoundsTrue.com you will find a wealth of free resources to support your journey, including exclusive weekly audio interviews, free downloads, interactive learning tools, and other special savings on all our titles.

To learn more, please visit SoundsTrue.com/freegifts or call us toll-free at 800-333-9185.

SOUNDS TRUE
many voices, one journey